Grayling

Bream

Carp

Tench

Pike

COARSE FISHING
A BEGINNER'S GUIDE

COARSE FISHING
A BEGINNER'S GUIDE

by

G. CARTWRIGHT

Illustrated by Baz East

LUTTERWORTH PRESS
LONDON

First published 1972
Second impression 1974

ISBN 0 7188 1675 7

Printed in Great Britain by Cox & Wyman Ltd.,
London, Fakenham and Reading

CONTENTS

5

Dedicated to my constant angling companion Peter Tennant, who safely transports me on all my fishing trips and drives home in a most wide awake condition; whilst I am apt to doze off and sometimes fall sound asleep!

LIST OF ILLUSTRATIONS

INTRODUCTION

IN sharp contrast to the majority of anglers who have written piscatorial tomes, I had a most frustrating start to my fishing career. My parents were very poor and had neither the time nor the cash to indulge me when, at the tender age of five, I began to think that my days were intended solely for the wonderous pursuit of angling and the nights for sleeping and dreaming about it!

However, despite the lack of appropriate gear in my early stages, I had lots of time; aeons of it, to watch endlessly the anglers sitting by river, lake or pond, to study carefully their tackle and methods, and question them everlastingly—if they were of sufficiently good nature.

I had devoured most of the books written by the 'Between Wars' angling authors by the time I was twelve but, from their writings, formed the impression that they were, as persons, rather highfalutin' and lacking in perception. They fondly imagined all their readers to be wealthy adults who could purchase all the specialized tackle they prescribed, as well as being sufficiently elevated on the social ladder to escape the irksome drudgery of having to turn out for work on five or six days of the week!

Here, I offer readers of all ages a down-to-earth book which caters specially for the coarse fishing beginner of strictly limited means and opportunity. Fishing is great fun and it should always be so, despite personal circumstances. Fish have no ability to differentiate between their captors—they pull heartily for millionaire and labourer alike.

Take heart all you second-hand department searchers. I am in my middle forties and have only just, in the last few years, been able to gather together what I would call a comprehensive set of decent tackle, most of which I have made myself. Nevertheless, my fishing has always been wonderfully enjoyable, despite the fact that for ages I had only the barest essentials of small tackle and just one rod and a reel.

9

CHAPTER 1

SOME OBSERVATIONS ON THE COARSE FISHING SCENE TODAY

IN this rushing, pushing, speed-mad world, I am happy to note that there are at least three or four million sensible souls, on this small island alone, who regularly go fishing whenever they can grab the chance in order to find peace and enjoy both mental and physical recuperation at the waterside.

As we are now well launched on a computerized, decimal weight, measurement and currency era, when we shall accept as commonplace the five, four and even three day working week, the younger generation who are interested in angling, can cheerfully look forward to a rosy future so far as leisure time is concerned. Water space will naturally present its problems, but I am sure these will be surmounted if we can only impress upon the people who control our destiny that angling is one of the most important of our national participant sports.

'Coarse' or 'Freshwater' fishing should not be confused with 'Game' fishing which is the catching of salmon and trout. Only the less delectable of our British freshwater fishes have been termed 'Coarse Fish'. The grayling is the one exception for although this is a member of the salmon family, it chooses to spawn at the same time as coarse fish—late spring and early summer—and can be caught during the recognized Coarse Fishing Season. This season is subject to local variations but generally runs from mid-June to mid-March.

There are many and varied waters on this island home of ours. Broad, deep rivers with a host of small shallower tributaries, feeder streams and overgrown backwaters. Meres and lakes, reservoirs, gravel pits, brickponds and in some parts of the country a veritable maze of slow flowing, lock controlled inland waterways, canals and drains. Before you even start to think of buying tackle, it is a wise plan to investigate all the fishing in your area and find out what the various waters have to offer. A survey such as this will most certainly give you an idea of the species and size of fish you are likely to catch and will ultimately be of great use when you begin to gather together some appropriate tackle.

A one-inch Ordnance Survey map is recommended when studying the country surrounding your home. This will enable you to pin-point every river, pond, drain or dyke (all marked in bright blue), to locate the position of bridges and also the nearness of roads and public footpaths. At present these maps cover 190 separate areas of Great Britain and offer the coarse fishing beginner an indispensable, accurate source of visual information.

Free fishing, in this modern day and age, is practically non-existent. Wherever you may wander to find water, it is customary to be confronted by notice boards, even in the most isolated places, which pronounce in clear terms that the fishing rights belong to some private person, angling club or syndicate. You may occasionally find an overgrown, neglected water, which appears to be derelict. Be warned . . . Do not fish without first attempting to find out who controls the water. A very embarrassing or painful experience could be the outcome of such foolishness. Remember, the onus is upon the angler to do the investigating before he fishes—and not the owner to seek him out and put him right.

A word here about the various different types of anglers who rejoice in the name 'Coarse Fishermen'. Unlike some politicians or football team supporters, they are certainly not violently opposed to each other —in fact quite a number of them are apt to have a foot in all camps and flit from one section to the other as the mood takes them.

I think by far the largest number are the 'Pleasure Anglers'. Newcomers to fishing will be rather mystified by this term. Surely all angling is pleasure? It is, but in order to differentiate between 'Match Anglers'—those who are taking part in organized fishing matches or competitions—and the footloose, roving fishermen who fish where and when they please, these two names have been coined. It is quite possible for a confirmed 'Match Angler' to be seen out on his own practising on a water where he will be competing in the near future. If questioned he would say that he was 'Pleasure Fishing', as though the 'Match Angling' was his work and this other kind of fishing his relaxation or fun and games.

The third group has come to be known, since about the beginning of the 1950s, as 'Specimen Hunters' or 'Big Fish Catchers'. This fraternity usually pool their knowledge and resources in order to improve the fish catching ability of their members. Utopia indeed!

'Specimen Hunters' are usually responsible for most of the large fish caught each season. They frequently fish in small groups of three or four and concentrate on one species in a chosen water for perhaps two or three seasons—to the exclusion of all other forms of angling. Theirs is usually a long, hard and often lonely path, one that only a few anglers would care to tread. However, this sport of ours has many facets—therefore each angler should at all times have the faith and perseverance to follow up his personal ideals.

Since motor cars are now used by the majority of the community, secluded stretches of river bank, remote lakes and off-the-beaten-track gravel pits are no longer the secret haunts of a few favoured fishermen. Nevertheless, the newcomer to our sport who is willing to walk a mile or so and hump his tackle over a stile or five barred gate can still be assured of getting himself quietly tucked away, far from his fellow humans, should he feel so inclined.

The 'family-man' casual angler, out in his car for the day with wife and children, will usually choose a picnic type of stopping place—a flat grassy area by a river, lake or stream—and remain there all the time, scarcely straying ten or twenty yards from base.

In distant times, now departed, when the five-and-a-half and six day week was the normal work stint, the Sabbath was nationally recognized as the great angling day. I abandoned it some time ago and now favour an all-day Saturday session. A friend of mine, who is somewhat proud of his anti-social habits, has secured himself a permanent night shift job so that he can fish mid-week afternoons and evenings in reasonable solitude.

When you are in the initial stages of trying to become a successful angler, it is very tempting to chase around all over the countryside, dabbling in each and every little bit of water you learn about or see written up in the angling press. However, I would strongly advise you to become thoroughly proficient on your home waters first, so that at least you can handle your tackle properly and make fairly consistent catches. This is the firm foundation you must lay in order to acquire the necessary concentration for what I will term 'difficult' fishing.

Before you even start to think in terms of money and tackle shops, spend at least a couple of sessions by the waterside in the company of some seasoned and truthful (they are not hard to find) angler. Watch him perform, take note of his gear and talk quietly to him. If he is not of the communicative kind just sit tight and watch; this is a very small price to pay for a free, expert demonstration.

Impatience at this stage is a very common failing. Very few prospective anglers can stem the first rush of mad enthusiasm which overwhelms them when they first discover the fascinating world of fishing. They all get an overriding obsession to rush off and buy some tackle—hang the expense and unsuitability of what they have chosen—and hot-foot it to the nearest water in order to get started.

Let us now consider one of the most controversial aspects of angling. The subject of waterside companions. Whether to fish alone and please yourself the whole time, or team up with perhaps just one or two others of similar interests and angle on a more or less co-operative basis. The latter method cuts down on travelling expenses, especially if three or four of you use one car and all chip in to a 'kitty' to cover petrol costs. Snags arise, of course, with this arrangement and I have personally found it not to my liking. The car owner usually has to set off very early and is quite often delayed as he invariably finds his passengers not quite ready for the 'off'. Sometimes they are still sound asleep! Insult is further added to injury on the journey back as the chauffeur is the very last to arrive home after dropping off all his charges one by one.

The time fixed for packing up is also liable to raise an argument. Some family men have wives who think all anglers should be home in time for a five o'clock tea. Conversely, I have, on a couple of occasions, journeyed to far places with hard drinking fishermen who worked up such a thirst on the riverbank, that they had a ritual pint in every one of the many pubs on the long drive home.

Youngsters suffer an even greater dilemma with the transport problem. Public service vehicles rarely take anglers to the outlandish places they would most like to go so pedal cycles and mopeds, which are both excellent for short distances, are used a great deal. They can be ridden along tow paths and beside ponds or pits if the banks are flat, provided you have not a great load of tackle to carry and the weather is fine. I know a couple of youths in their early teens who have worked out admirable arrangements with their parents for fishing trips. One gets set down every Sunday by his family who are *en route* to the seaside, and picked up again in the evening when they return. The other has a gem of a father who rises early, dons an overcoat over his pyjamas and drives him to the fishing venue. He returns home to finish his Sunday lie-in and then brings his son back again at night!

Whoever you choose to angle with, try to make sure his enthusiasm for the game matches yours. If you like to pack up and call it a day when it turns cold or starts to rain then get someone of the same mind. If you have to be home at a specified hour to watch your favourite programme on the 'Telly' or visit the club, a bingo hall or the cinema then steer clear of fanatics like me who are prepared to linger on at the waterside all through the night if the fish keep on feeding.

Seriously, if you have any doubts about waterside companions when you first start to fish, go it alone for a few visits. You may be surprised to find that at heart you are a lone wolf—completely happy by yourself.

CHAPTER 2

ACQUIRING SOME SUITABLE TACKLE

W HEN the fishing bug first bit me badly, I had lots of time to find out what sort of tackle I required but alas, very little money to buy it with. Each treasured item was painfully saved for and bought breathlessly as soon as the exact sum of money had been raised. Whilst I do not wish such harrowing experiences upon my readers, I unwittingly followed the right path. Buy only the bare necessities at first then diligently practise as many times as you can until you can fish with them effortlessly.

The tackle shops of today are packed with a bewildering conglomeration of eye-catching gear in a price range that is often puzzling. How, then, can the absolute beginner with money to spend, successfully choose what is most suitable to his needs and come away with a correct selection of the right items at a fair price?

There are three very simple answers:

1. Take your time and gather together all the tackle catalogues, trade hand-outs and leaflets available and study them, noting prices, rod lengths, reel specifications; then visit as many big 'walk-round' tackle shops as you can find before you buy.

2. Find an angling friend who will guide you on the right path when you make your initial purchases.

3. March into a well-known tackle shop run by a practical angler (at a slack period, such as a Monday morning, he will welcome you with open arms) and tell him what you have to spend and where you intend to fish.

Combine all these three and I am positive you will get everything correct.

Rods for Coarse Fishing

If you have studied the manufacturers' and agents' catalogues or made visits to tackle showrooms, you will find that coarse fishing rods come in a wide variety of prices, materials, lengths, actions and purpose types. Lately there has been a tremendous amount of fashion conscious-ness displayed by otherwise level-headed anglers where rods are con-cerned. If the present trend continues we shall soon emulate the motor car industry and have everyone turning in his tackle every year for a fresh set of 'This Year's' model! Whilst I abhor this status symbol atti-tude in the angling world, I must admit it is healthy from a trade point of view; more important, every close season, there seem to be many very good, hardly used rods going at rock-bottom prices. (New starters of limited means kindly take note.)

Rods that are constructed from natural, round cane (bottom two pieces) and solid fibre glass (top piece) are the cheapest and usually the heaviest you can buy. They are quite often in three 3 ft. 6 in. joints and make up to about 10 ft. in length. Their weight is on the heavy side, 16 to 20 oz. These rods, when well constructed, with good quality rings, ferrules and a decent cork handle with sliding reel fittings, are quite a reasonable buy. Immediately above these 'beginners' or 'boys' rods, in the middle price bracket, are the cheaper of the custom-made 'Match' and general purpose 'Avon' rods. These come in built (split) cane or hollow glass. The term 'Match Rod' or 'Avon' refers to the 'action' or curve of the rod when it bends to the resistance of a fish being played or brought in through the water.

Match anglers generally require a 'tip-action' in their rods. This allows a quick strike or flick of the wrist to set the hook. As match anglers normally don't reckon on taking very big fish, but lots of small and medium-sized ones in rapid succession, it is only necessary for the top part of the rod to bend. The 'Avon' rod is totally different. It has what is called a softer 'through' action and a tip that is much less whippy than a 'Match Rod'. It bends well down into the second joint pro-ducing a greater curve when flexed, which has a cushioning effect that prevents a really big fish making a sudden plunge and snapping the line.

You will find that the 'Match' rods are apt to be quite a bit longer than the 'Avon' types. Match anglers like their rods between 12 and 14½ ft., whilst the 'Avon' or general purpose coarse fishing rods are either in 2 pieces for the nine, ten and eleven footers, or in the traditional three pieces for those that are 12 ft. and over.

In the top bracket of the price list come the high-class specialist 'Name Rods' in the very best quality split cane and hollow glass. Lots of very famous, well respected big fish catchers and match anglers of proved ability lend their names to the rods in this category. Name rods have been designed after many experiments under actual fishing conditions and manufactured from high-class materials to stringent specifications. If you can afford one of these 'name' rods, you will have an item of tackle which is a wonderful example of the rod maker's art—a sheer joy to use and a friend for life.

To sum up. If most of your fishing is to be done with light float tackle on small canals, drains, narrow slow-flowing rivers, shallow ponds and lakes where the fish do not appear to run very large and the catch will consist of roach, perch and perhaps a few bream, any 'match' type rod of about 12 ft. will admirably to start with.

In direct contrast, should your home area be blessed with broad, deep 'whopper filled' rivers, holding chub and barbel, or vast gravel pits and lakes in which lurk monster roach, perch, tench and bream— your fishing will be of the heavier style and an 'Avon' rod ought to be your choice.

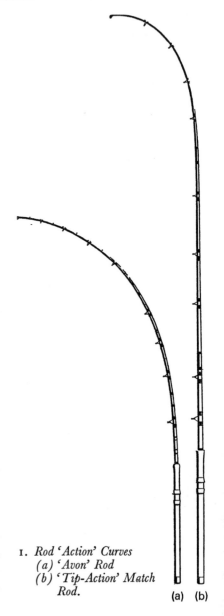

1. *Rod 'Action' Curves*
   (a) 'Avon' Rod
   (b) 'Tip-Action' Match Rod.

(a) (b)

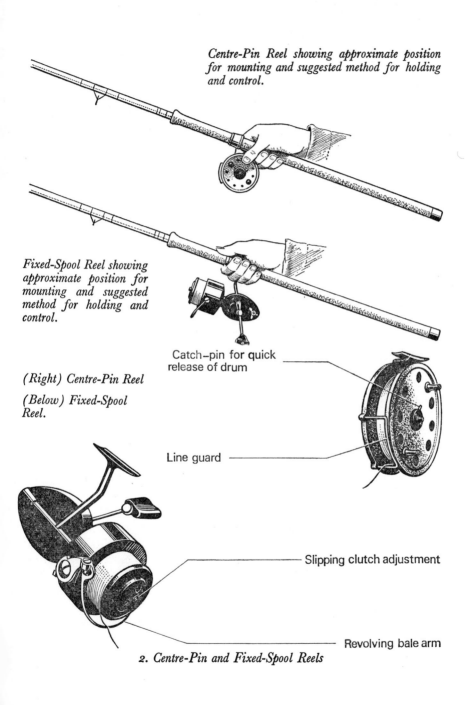

Centre-Pin Reel showing approximate position for mounting and suggested method for holding and control.

Fixed-Spool Reel showing approximate position for mounting and suggested method for holding and control.

(Right) Centre-Pin Reel

(Below) Fixed-Spool Reel.

Catch–pin for quick release of drum

Line guard

Slipping clutch adjustment

Revolving bale arm

2. Centre-Pin and Fixed-Spool Reels

A good quality rod should feel light in the hand and weigh between 8 to 16 oz. according to length and material. It should have well-fitting ferrules that go right home on assembly and do not stick when the rod is dismantled, a slim handle of good quality cork between 24 and 30 in., plenty of well spaced, neatly whipped rings and a sectioned bag of durable material. The maker is very proud to show his name on such a rod as this. It will invariably appear in transfer form just above the cork handle, with details of weight and length and usually a facsimile signature of the angler who has designed it.

Reels

Now we hit the problems and begin to learn about angling controversies. When considering the purchase of a coarse fishing reel, you will find that there are two quite dissimilar types generally used and each kind has its strong devotees. One is the fixed-spool reel, with its single, large, offset handle, revolving bale arm and spool 'end-on', at right angles to the rod; the other is the traditional centre-pin, revolving, narrow drum reel, with two small knobs or handles and usually an interchangeable line guard for right or left-hand use.

One dragon which needs immediate slaying is the age old balderdash about reels being 'married' or 'balanced' to rods. I use both fixed-spool and centre-pin reels and have never ever considered the 'one reel to one rod' myth. Each of my reels gets used on all of my rods at various times according to fishing conditions and my personal whims.

How about an all-round reel for the beginner? As a 'Centre-Pin Exponent', I would make the somewhat surprising recommendation that you first get a fixed-spool reel, then, when you have mastered it, go on to a centre-pin for different kinds of angling. In other words you will end up like me—using both!

Time now to consider another angling 'bogey'. The 'which hand shall I use the rod with?' problem. This must be decided early. Unless it has an interchangeable handle, the fixed-spool reel which I suggest you buy, should have either a left or right-hand wind. This will have the handle sticking out on the left or right-hand side of the reel when it is correctly mounted and the spool facing towards the rod end, below the cork grip.

If you are right handed you will, I am sure, find it most convenient to use the rod in that hand and operate the reel with your left hand.

Therefore get a left-hand wind reel. For left handers, the reverse will apply. Once you begin fishing you will observe quite a number of anglers doing all sorts of swap-over hand techniques which will be puzzling until you realize that although they cast with the rod in one hand, they change hands once they have done so, because they can't get out of the habit of trying to operate both rod and reel with the same hand. Try not to follow their example or you will become what I call 'a one-armed fisherman'.

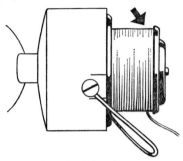

3. *Filling Fixed-Spool Drum correctly with line.*

In order to put you in the picture, I will list the advantages and drawbacks of the two types of reels so that you will be able to form your own opinions and decide if you agree with my ideas about this all important item of tackle.

A fixed-spool reel, by virtue of its design, has a non-revolving spool with the line being drawn over the lip when casting. If the spool is loaded with line to within an eighth of an inch of the lip (as per illustration) it will give you instant casting distance without lots of arduous practice. The price will not be too formidable and usually includes a spare spool for a different breaking strain of line. The reel's slipping clutch mechanism, which can be set to give line when the breaking strain is being approached, will extricate you from awkward situations in your first 'ham-fisted' stage.

Centre-pin reels are wonderful pieces of fishing tackle in the hands of experts. Their correct use is, without doubt, a fine art. The good ones are costly and have only the one drum for one strength of line. They require much diligent practise before long casts can be made. Sensitive control of the line for 'long trotting' (letting float tackle be borne down stream on a river by the 'pull' or flow of the current) and fish playing is possible; the fingers of both hands can be used to 'feel' the drum and can give line, clamp down tight or retrieve line, according to the antics of the fish and its nearness to weedbeds or underwater snags and obstructions.

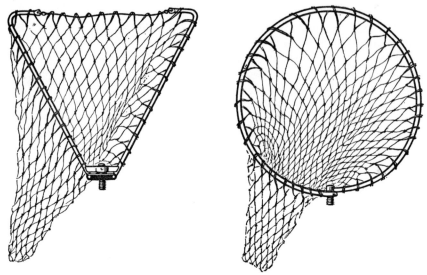

4. 'Apex' and Circular Landing Net Head types.

Landing nets

Having dealt with the two most expensive items in the coarse fishing beginner's list of essential tackle, let us now approach the joyful stage where we are thinking in terms of getting our catch on to the bank! It is safe to assume, I am sure, that the days of the extra strong rods and lines, which were capable of pulley-hauling any fish, however large, straight out of the water and up into the air over the angler's head, are happily, now long departed. The fine, well-balanced

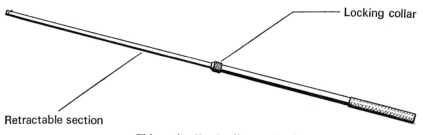

Locking collar

Retractable section

5. Telescopic alloy landing net handle.

fishing gear of today is primarily intended to afford great sport to the skilful angler; therefore it must always be remembered that the bodily lifting of the 'dead' weight of a good fish out of water is a thing to be avoided. The landing net takes care of this operation.

Basically there are two kinds of landing net on the market at the present time. The round framed type and the 'Apex' or triangular shaped. All three parts—frame, net and handle—can be purchased separately to give the buyer exactly what he requires. The frames are sold in varying sizes ranging from the smallest at 14 in. (suitable for small roach, perch, etc.) to the salmon, pike, barbel and carp catcher's frame, which is usually triangular and of a capacious 3 ft. size across the gape, where the two sides spread to their fullest extent.

The 'net' part should be deep and roomy at the bottom. It is produced by the tackle manufacturers in various colours, sizes and depths, from the synthetic materials Courlene, Terylene, Nylon and Ulstron. Some of them are very strong and fine, but alas, terribly harsh to the touch—avoid them—your catch will be mutilated and suffer from rough, abrasive treatment in a net of this kind. Landing-net handles come in all shapes and sizes, from the plain 4 or 5 ft. length of thick bamboo with a standard threaded cap which takes the landing-net screw, to the very latest and more expensive telescopic light alloy kind, that will enable you to reach out 8 or 9 ft. down a steep bank or over clumps of rushes and weedbeds.

Keep Nets

I think landing nets are essential, but I would say that the fewer keep nets that are used the better. Why do I list them, then? Sometimes they are a necessary evil. To the match angler, they are like life insurance.

When you visit tackle shops, you can't fail to notice keep nets. My tackle dealer hangs them up near his door and I bang my head on them. I think he is cunning and places them in this position so as to deter anyone who may harbour the evil intention of rushing out without paying!

Buy the largest size you can afford and a bank stick, threaded the same standard size as your landing net, to go with it. Wash it in warm water and dry it thoroughly after each outing (landing nets should get the same treatment) and above all, remember not to stuff it too full of fish.

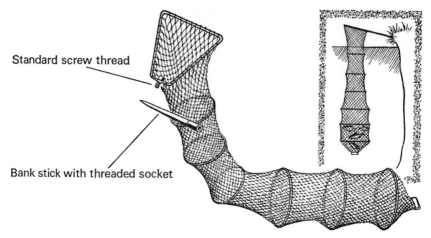

Standard screw thread

Bank stick with threaded socket

6. *Large Keep Net with Screw Bank Stick (inset) ideal position for use.*

Baskets, Tackle Carriers and Seats

These are the last of the large items before we consider all the other small stuff that completes our angling equipment. A comfortable seat is a vital necessity to any aspiring coarse fisherman. The very nature of this kind of angling demands long hours of sitting, watching and waiting without undue movement. This is a physical impossibility if you are not in a comfortable relaxed position on a firm, reliable seat. Note I mention 'reliable'. I once heard the agonized yells of a beefy gent who had his posterior painfully trapped in a natty folding stool when it collapsed on him unexpectedly!

Baskets are rated high on my list. They are reasonably cheap, very strong, not too heavy and stand a lot of rough usage. The bigger you buy them, the more you will be tempted to carry around and the quieter you will sit—too fatigued to fidget about! A good one built of extra strong unvarnished cane—willow is far more popular but not so durable—with four stout corner-post feet and a broad strap, will provide its owner with a comfortable seat for many years.

Rucksacks have their followers—just dump everything in and strap a folding seat to the outside. Tubular steel combined seat and tackle

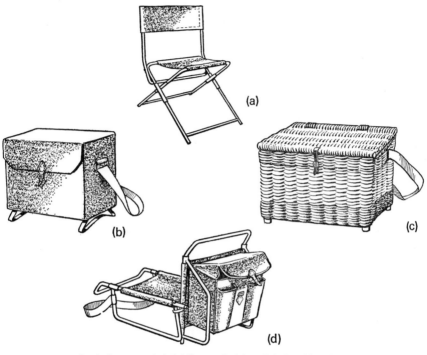

7. *Angler's seats.* *(a)* *'Adjusta-chair'* *(b)* *Combination seat and tackle carrier* *(c)* *Basket seat* *(d)* *Pakaseat.*

carriers are also on the market and are a very sound buy if your finances will run to one.

The best seat-cum-tackle-box I have ever seen was created by a joiner, who designed the whole thing to his own personal taste. It was made around a hardwood frame and the material used was marine, resin bonded plywood. The lift-up seat flap was luxuriously upholstered in thick foam rubber with a spongeable, waterproof covering. I enquired from the owner and found the outlay for the materials to be very cheap. It is the labour costs which put up the price of shop bought articles. Therefore, if you are a handyman type searching for a low-cost seat, tailored to your personal requirements, solve the problem by purchasing some wood and do the construction work yourself.

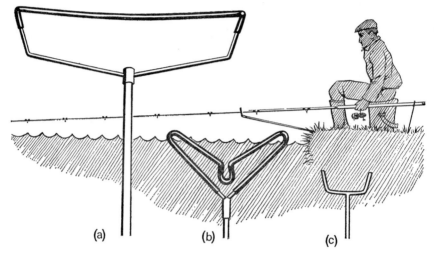

(a)　　　　　　　(b)　　　　　　　(c)

8. *Rod Rests. (a) Match type　(b) 'Specimen Hunter'*
(c) Back Rest (background illustration)
Angler—Rod Rest positions.

Rod Rests

Two correctly designed rod rests are essential. There are a wide variety available in tubular steel, with both plastic, metal and rubber rod holders. The front one should be long enough to reach out well over the water's edge and the rod holder broad enough to allow the angler to put the rod down without having to fit it carefully into a narrow groove. The back one is shorter and the rod holder smaller, so that it does not catch the angler's rod arm or sleeve. The 'Specimen Hunting' fraternity have designed a very special front rod rest which does not trap or impede free passage of the line when a taking fish 'runs' off with the baited hook. This is used in conjunction with a fixed-spool reel with the bale arm in the 'open' or 'off' position.

Line

Nylon monofilament has revolutionized angling. It is cheap, fine in relation to its strength and requires very little care and attention. For general coarse fishing, when you will be catching roach, perch, rudd, dace, bream and perhaps small chub, start off with a breaking strain of about 3 or 4 lb. Many very good 'delicate handed' anglers will be horrified by this suggestion, but until you learn to manage your tackle properly in strong winds and wet weather, a stiffer, thicker line will keep irritating tangles down to the minimum. If you happen to get a fixed-spool reel with a great deep line trough in the spool fill it up with some fine string first, so that the hundred yards of nylon you have bought just tops it up nicely to within about an eighth of an inch of the lip (as previously suggested). This precaution will facilitate long, easy casting.

Hooks

Hooks, although very small items, are actually of paramount importance and they should never be bought haphazardly in cheap job lots. Here again, I am sorry to relate, the coarse fishing world is apt to be divided, with the loose-hook 'tie them direct to the reel line' school on one side and the 'manufacturer tied, hooks to nylon, in transparent packet' crowd on the other.

Eyed and 'spade-end' hooks are cheap in relation to those that come attached to nylon. If they are fine in the wire and not coarse in the barb, and have well formed 'eyes' and 'spades', they are a sound, economical buy. Manufactured yard bottoms or hook links are apt to be infuriating as the line strength always seems to be strictly related to the hook size. Thick, strong line for big hooks and fine, gossamer stuff for the tiny ones is a good rule to follow although this uniformity is not always practicable during actual fishing.

Whatever your final choice, make sure you get an initial stock of a dozen of each size from 18 (the smallest) to about 6 or 8 (the largest). These will at least enable you to commence fishing, after which you will probably have many bankside chats with other anglers and form your own ideas about hooks and other items of your tackle. Eventually, you could end up as fanatical as I am where hooks are concerned, and swear by 'spade-end, crystal, gold-plated, flat-forged, short-shanked, Mustads'.

Study carefully the illustrations and instructions for tying the 'Domhof' knot, which will enable you to attach spade-end hooks to your line neatly and very securely. The half-blood knot for attaching eyed hooks to nylon monofilament is also a proved favourite with anglers. Practise tying each of these knots with thick string on a fork handle (to simulate a large 'spade-end') and the hand holes on a pair of scissors (they will serve as outsize hook eyes) until you reach a state of proficiency which will allow you to progress to fine nylon and small hooks.

The full-blood knot is very widely used by fishermen for joining lengths of nylon line of the same and varying thicknesses. It is invaluable when 'scaling-down' hook lengths or weight attachment links with nylon of a weaker breaking strain than the 'main' reel line. This avoids heavy terminal tackle losses when fishing snaggy swims.

As we are on the subject of hooks, I will explain the pitfalls of rash purchase to those who do not have unlimited funds at their disposal. For instance, a dozen each of 'hooks to nylon' in the six sizes from 18 to 8 (they step down in even numbers from about 20 to size 2) gives a total

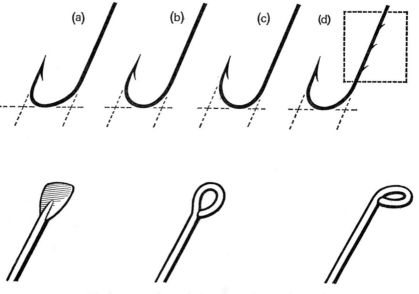

9. *Hook types. Top (a) Crystal   (b) Model Perfect*
(c) Round Bend   (d) Bait-holder shank
Below (left to right): Spade, Straight-
Eye, Turned-Down Eye.

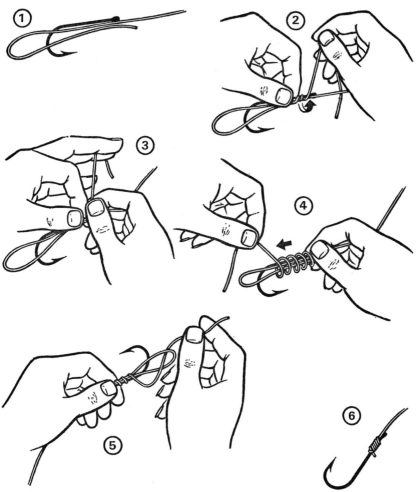

10. *Tying the 'Domhof' Knot.*

1. *Lay loop along hook shank.*
2. *Holding loop firmly against shank with forefinger and thumb of left hand, pass free end of line two or three times round shank.*
3. *Taking the free end between middle fingers of left hand, hold whipping secure with forefinger and thumb of right hand.*
4. *Whip six or seven turns down shank towards bend of hook.*
5. *Pass free end through loop.*
6. *Pull tight, slide knot up to nestle on the inside of shank against spade and snip off loose end.*

of six dozen hooks, which would cost about ten times as much as a box containing 50 assorted eyed hooks (ten each of five different sizes).

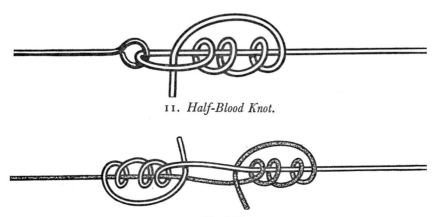

11. *Half-Blood Knot.*

12. *Blood Knot.*

Floats

These eye-catching, multi-coloured items of tackle are apt to turn the brain of all but the most self-disciplined angler, so that he ends up with a large, expensive collection of floats, only a few of which he ever uses. Your choice should be governed strictly by the type of waters in which you intend fishing. Broadly speaking, big, deep, fast waters need large floats capable of carrying a heavy shot load whilst, in direct contrast, the shallow, narrow canals, slow flowing rivers and small ponds and lakes, require lighter floats that need only a few small split-shot to cock them.

Fashions in floats have changed almost beyond recognition during the past few years. There was a time when crow, goose, swan and porcupine quills (with or without cork barrels) reigned supreme in the float fisher's tackle box. Today, balsa and cane stemmed creations are all the rage and there is such a perplexing array of self-cockers, duckers, sliders, antennae and stick-floats available that the poor angling tyro would be well advised to start his fishing with a bare half-dozen. A couple of 6 or 7 in. porcupine quills and 3 or 4 of the cane stemmed, balsa or cork jacketed pattern, in different sizes is an ideal selection.

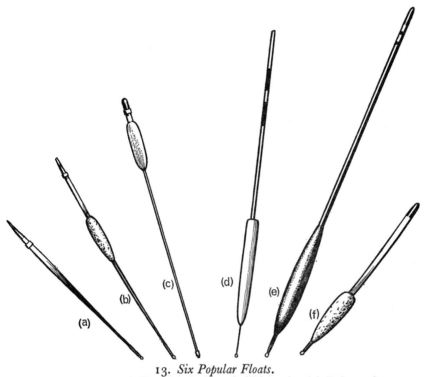

13. *Six Popular Floats.*
(a) Porcupine Quill   (b) Cork on Quill 'Avon'   (c) Balsa and wire-stemmed 'Trotter'   (d) Bottom Ring Slider   (e) Antenna (f) Cork on Quill 'Ducker'.

Additions can and, I am sure, will be made just as soon as the angler has got a few visits to the water under his belt and begins to feel he understands his fishing.

Split-shot

These are the small, round pieces of sliced lead that are nipped on to the line underneath the float between it and the hook to make the float stand upright in the water and get the bait down to the required depth. Since split-shots originated from actual shotgun pellets, when they were split by hand with a knife and adapted to angling, the sizes by which they are known correspond to the shotgun pellet gradations. The largest are 'swanshot', then, coming down in size, there are AA and BB—the very smallest being 'dust-shot'.

A circular plastic dispenser, with six or seven separate compartments holding a range of split-shot sizes from large to very small, can be bought quite cheaply. This supply will last indefinitely provided the box is not trodden into the bank or knocked into the water. Split-shots are only a small item but their condition, like that of hooks, is of great importance. They should be made of very soft, dull lead, and the 'splits'

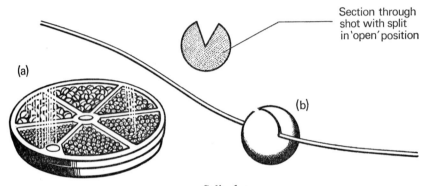

14. *Split-shot.*
(a) Assorted Size Dispenser   (b) Method of attaching to line.

should be clean cut and central. Ignore the label on the box which may state 'Soft Split-Shot' and give them what I call the 'thumb-nail test'. Nip one between your teeth until the slit is closed tight, then attempt to slide your thumb nail into the groove to open it up again. If this cannot be done, don't buy the shot—it is much too hard!

Your teeth should leave impressions on the right kind of soft shot which should never have to be nipped on to the line with pliers. Such treatment crushes the nylon monofilament which is quite soft, and weakens it a great deal.

Plummet

Although some quite knowledgeable anglers will scoff at the mere suggestion of using one of these depth finders, I always use one when float fishing so that I can form a mental picture of the swim or the angling spot where I intend to fish. They are quite cheap so buy two as I am sure you will accidentally drop one into the water on your very first angling trip. There are several refined forms of plummet available in clip-on and instant release styles, but the basic pattern is also quite good. This is simply a conical shaped lead weighing an ounce or so, with a brass ring set in the top and a piece of cork inserted into a slit in the bottom.

When the tackle has been assembled, but before the shot has been put on the line, pass the hook through the ring of the plummet and secure by nick-ing the point into the cork. Set the float at the estimated depth and swing the tackle out to the spot where you intend to fish. If the float is pulled under by the plum-met sinking to the bottom, you should slide the float up the line, away from the plummet, until the stage is reached where the plummet is resting on the bottom and the float just stands with its tip clear of the water. You have now ascertained

15. *Method of attaching plum-met with hook point in cork insert.*

the exact depth of that part of the water. Plop the plummet in an-other half - dozen times, a little farther out and to each side of you. There may be a deep hole on one side where the float suddenly sinks out of view and perhaps a shelf on the other where the float stops following the plummet and lays flat on the surface of the water with perhaps a couple of feet of line lying slack.

The plummet will tell you all you want to know about the bottom contours. After you have plumbed the exact depth of your fishing spot, you can then adjust your float to fish with the bait either lying right on the bottom, just above it, or suspended in mid-water.

Disgorger

Every angler, I am sure, likes to hook all his fish cleanly in the top or bottom lip so that the hook shank just protrudes from the mouth of the fish. This makes for an easy removal with the thumb and forefinger. Things do not always go strictly to plan and due to various causes—

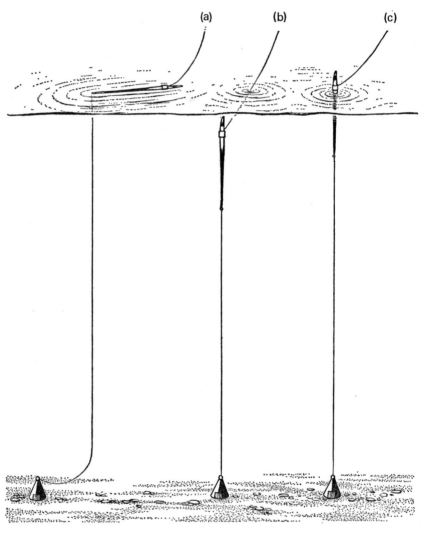

16. *Plumming the Depth.*
(a) Too deep   (b) Too shallow   (c) Just right.

slow-thinking anglers or fast-biting fish—the hook may be out of sight or deeply embedded in the mouth of the fish. It is then that a disgorger is required.

The simplest, cheapest kind is nothing more than a seven or eight-inch piece of round metal, flattened at one end, with a 'v' slot cut into it. I do not like them. Poking around in the innards of the fish with those two fork-like prongs produces all kinds of bad after effects and damage. Sometimes the careless use of one of these crude instruments causes the swim bladder of the fish to be punctured and a slow, painful death results. Only a little better are the blunt ended 'slotted' disgorgers. These have no 'prongs' but still require a prodding, poking action to be effective. Surgical artery forceps are the ideal unhooking tool. Although rather pricey, they do a wonderful, humane unhooking job and are worth the extra cash expended.

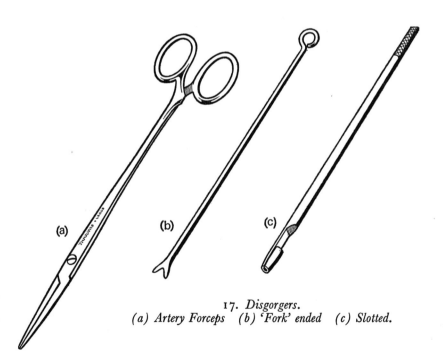

17. *Disgorgers.*
(a) Artery Forceps   (b) 'Fork' ended   (c) Slotted.

Bait Boxes

Tins with nail holes in the lids for worm and maggot receptacles are, luckily, a thing of the past. They rusted, they rattled, and the maggots and worms escaped through the over large holes. Modern plastics have provided the answers to many angling problems and bait boxes in unbreakable polythene, which are rust, tread and clang proof, are a great boon.

Initially, buy a couple, one for worms, the other for maggots. When you become a seasoned angler, you will probably have a collection of half-dozen, all containing separate deadly baits!

Groundbait Mixing Bowls and Hand Towels

There is no need to pay out good money for these two items. A crafty hunt around the kitchen-sink area will bring to light a small, shallow polythene washing-up bowl, and also a dark coloured (it will be even darker later on) towel which is slightly tatty and almost ready for the rag-bag.

That just about completes the basic essentials of a coarse fishing outfit. As I look over my own selection of tackle, I just dare not reveal what I have amassed. All sorts of attractive and useful objects come to light which I fondly imagine I couldn't possibly do without. Some items are not really vital but they do make for greater angling pleasure and comfort. Here are a few extra items, both large and small, which every angling beginner will wish to own sooner or later. However, don't lash out on these and skimp on your rod and reel—that would be false economy.

Holdalls

It is wonderfully convenient to be able to carry your treasured rod, rests, landing-net handle, umbrella and landing-net head in a properly designed shoulder sling bag. A good stiffened rod holdall is ideal. It protects the contents, keeps them dry and saves you from losing them when staggering along a muddy riverbank in the dark. Rod holdalls are manufactured in strong, rotproof canvas or leather-grained PVC.

There are three usual measurements, $4\frac{1}{2}$, 5 and $5\frac{1}{2}$ ft. long. The cost will vary considerably according to the quality, size and number of separate rod, landing net and umbrella pockets.

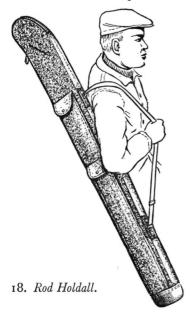

18. *Rod Holdall.*

Umbrellas

An angling friend of mine, who shall be nameless, puts his views about fishing umbrellas in a few very well chosen words. "In this climate, get a brolly before you even buy a rod!" Those are not my sentiments but I must admit that I have often erected my umbrella to keep off a cold wind, even in the height of summer, so for real comfort I suppose you could say they are the angler's life saver.

Do not economize if you intend buying one. The smallest have 36 in. ribs and are just not big enough to protect you and your tackle in

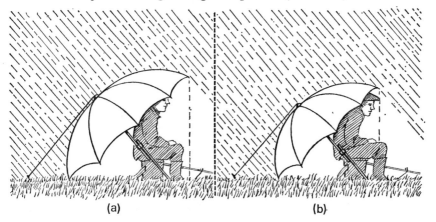

(a) (b)

19. *Umbrellas.*
(a) 42"—comfortable (b) 36"— Angler hunched up with water dripping on his knees.

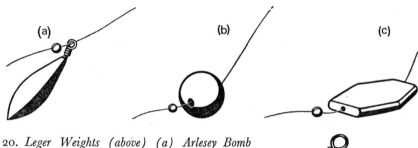

20. *Leger Weights (above) (a) Arlesey Bomb (b) Drilled bullet (c) Coffin lead.*

21. *A selection of Swivels (right) (a) Barrel (b) American 'Snap' (c) Link Swivel.*

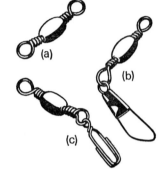

a downpour. They might appear huge when opened in the close confines of a tackle shop, but do not be misled. Only in a few circumstances can they be erected in an upright position directly over the angler's head. When they are tilted at an angle, with one side touching the ground, they don't extend far enough over the seated angler's head which means that the rain drips off into the tops of his wellington boots, all over his knees and, if he is an outsize man, right down the back of his neck! Size 42 in. ribs are essential. They give that extra six inches all round that is often the difference between being steadily dripped upon or being bone dry. For the very big man, or those anglers who feel the cold acutely, the extra large 45 in. ribbed umbrellas are a blessing, but remember, they must be very securely pegged down in a high wind.

Incidental Small Tackle

Here is a list of items that are always useful:

(a) A sharp penknife, one sided razor blade, scissors or nail clippers for trimming the ends of knots in nylon line.

(b) Spring balance to get the reasonably accurate weight of any 'monsters' you catch.

38

(c) Tape measure for ascertaining length and girth of large fish.

(d) Assorted leger weights of the 'coffin', 'Arlesey Bomb' and 'Bored Bullet' pattern from ⅛ oz. to 1 oz., together with a selection of small swivels and plenty of swan shot.

(e) A 4 in. steel bladed paint stripper which will prove its worth when a tilting basket or box seat threatens to tip you headlong into the water.

(f) Cycle valve tubing. Cut into small pieces, this makes excellent float rings. Floats when purchased usually have a rubber ring on them but invariably it has perished due to being stretched and left on the float. Store these valve rubber rings in a small box and take them off each float after it has been used.

(g) Rubber waterproof torch. This is an insurance against delaying your packing-up time until after dark when it is too late to see your tackle or find your way safely from the water's edge.

Conclusion

If your tackle buying is to be done on a strict budget, look around a bit before you actually buy. Try to contact any angling friends you may have and see if they have some good, second-hand tackle for sale. Fishermen are a rare brotherhood and great favours come as second nature to them. Don't suffer the shocking indignity of proudly displaying a quite expensive rod to one of your angling pals and be instantly deflated when he calmly says: "Oh! dear, I'm sorry to hear you have bought one of those. I could have let you have one for half the price!"

CHAPTER 3

THE WATERS WHERE WE SHALL FISH

WHEN considering the waters in which our fishing is to be done, we can allow ourselves the broad generalization of dividing them roughly into two distinct types: running, and still waters.

Ultimately, all rivers and their tributaries of smaller rivers and feeder streams, flow into the sea. However, in times of drought, when the water levels are very low, this movement may be so feeble and sluggish that temporarily the river would appear to be a still water. Likewise, on rivers which are controlled throughout their entire length by a system of lock gates or sluices, the flow can be controlled to such an extent that the waters will be allowed to roar along in times of heavy rainfall (to prevent flooding), and held back and conserved when the climatic conditions have been exceptionally dry.

The term 'still water' is usually given to ponds, lakes, meres, reservoirs, gravel pits and non-tidal broads and lochs. Some disused canals and inland waterways which flow into rivers, must also be included for they have ceased to be used for navigation purposes and have been allowed to become overgrown, badly silted up and weed choked. The somewhat loose description 'still', for the aforementioned waters, is sometimes a grave misnomer. Still waters are seldom what their name implies. Surface drift caused by wind, the bubbling up of underwater springs and currents beneath the surface all perpetuate motion in the water. To the casual bankside observer these movements are unseen, but the angler soon becomes aware of them and finds himself so intrigued that he begins to study them, often unconsciously.

Of special importance to anglers dwelling in the Eastern Counties is the vast network of Fenland rivers, drains and dykes which have a slow flowing character of their very own. Situated in the flat, low-lying district surrounding the Wash, they represent a perfect habitat for those species of coarse fish which love sluggish water. They draw anglers like a magnet from far and near.

From all these observations and the study of a large-scale map of his immediate locality, the prospective coarse fisher will be able to find out what types of fishing waters are available to him. One big question which poses itself at this stage is the age old angling dilemma suffered by all beginners—what kind of fish can I expect to catch?

Again, the rough and ready guide of running and still waters can be called upon to assist with this problem. Some fish breed and thrive in both of these environments, others do not.

Barbel, dace, chub and grayling are the four 'running water' fish which immediately spring to mind. I would not be so rashly pedantic as to express the opinion that they could not exist in clean, still water, but it is extremely doubtful whether they would thrive, breed and give good sport when hooked.

Eels appear to be ubiquitous. There are very few waters which do not hold them. Pike, perch, roach and rudd inhabit both still and running waters and seem equally at home in either. Bream, carp and tench are primarily still water species but also prosper in a slow-flowing river or canal environment wherein they usually wax exceedingly fat and give a good account of themselves at the end of a line.

Rivers

I would not advise the coarse fishing beginner to make his debut on a wide, fast-flowing river, owing to the difficulty he would initially experience of controlling his tackle correctly. However, the best of our coarse fish holding rivers do represent an endless challenge to the experienced, skilful angler who can often take wonderful catches from them. Alas, this fishing always needs careful study and a patient approach as rivers are for ever subject to the vagaries of the weather.

Heavy rainfall, for just a short period, will turn some rivers into a raging, cocoa coloured torrent almost overnight, whilst a prolonged drought, reduces the once sparkling flow to a scum laden trickle. In either of these conditions the angler is faced with an annoying natural hazard before he even wets a line.

Running waters produce a very fit, hard fighting brand of fish. These waters usually fish well in the winter months and do not freeze except in really Arctic temperatures.

Of paramount importance to the river fishermen is that magical 'sixth sense' ability known as 'reading the water'. River-keepers, water bailiffs and those anglers who take the time and trouble to attune themselves to nature, develop this 'water reading' ability to an uncanny degree which leaves the ordinary layman astounded. To walk the riverbank with someone intimately acquainted with it, is an education which no amateur angler should miss if the chance is offered.

Rivers do not just flow steadily in a downstream direction, and the fish in them are rarely distributed evenly. There are slacks and eddies, backflows, glides, shallow fast runs, and deep, quiet pools. Locating his quarry is usually the hardest part of the angler's task. Sun glasses with polarizing lenses which cut down the water-surface glare are indispensable as they enable the angler to view clear water right through down to the bottom. A stealthy approach, often on hands and knees, gives the best results. Just blithely strolling along the edge of the bank, in full view, is a complete and utter waste of time when fish locating is being taken seriously. The bankside vibrations caused by regular, heavy footfalls, and the large looming shape of an angler will usually put all the denizens of the river on their guard and cause them to 'melt' quietly away into the weedbeds.

Deep, muddy rivers or those in which the water is densely clouded with suspended matter, present problems which are often insurmountable. If the only indications to be seen are those taking place on the surface, it is doubly difficult to form an idea of what is also going on down below. In this case, 'fish watching' changes to 'angler watching', so that some idea of what is caught, where and when, can be obtained.

When barbel are present in a river they will usually be found in the well oxygenated stretches among the streamer weed which trails in profusion over the stony or gravelly runs. They can also be found in deep weirpools, where they love to hug the bottom in the fast water and feed on the many and varied aquatic morsels borne down by the current. River pike will frequently share some of the spots chosen by the barbel, but they also hunt and harry roach and dace shoals in shallow water. They lie in ambush in the quiet slacks from where they rush out into the main stream to seize their prey as it swims past. Perch have a liking for deep holes, the areas around jetties, piles and lock gates, as well as for undercut banks where there are tree roots.

Chub are great lovers of overhanging bushes and bankside vegetation.

In summer they can be seen just below the surface waiting to gulp down the various insects which fall from these overhead larders. They also revel in snaggy weirpools and the long 'live water' glides below them, where they can be seen feeding splashily on the endless offerings of food carried down by the current, or chasing minnows and other small fish into the shallows.

Small and medium 'shoal size' dace and roach are fairly well spread out in rivers and their location is seldom difficult. However, it is a piscatorial art to find any of the big specimens, necessitating great study of their habits and the water conditions, not to mention, at times, an outsize slice of luck! Big roach and dace like a sand or gravel bottom, plenty of weed growth and clean water. Once you have found a shoal of breathtaking monsters, do not be deluded into thinking that all they need is a baited hook in the right place! Such fish do not attain their great size by foolish living.

Look for river rudd near the surface, in the vicinity of reeds and lily-pads, during the summer months. But once the October and November frosts have blackened and withered the reed stems, and the bankside growth is dying off, seek them in deeper water.

If your local rivers are slow flowing and inclined to be muddy, then they will most probably contain bream. Together with small roach, dace and perch, they make up the bulk of the match angler's catch. In your initial coarse fishing stages you will most probably take some without difficulty, and this first success will do a great deal towards bolstering your ego and make you keen for further waterside outings.

Do not feel deeply disappointed if your favourite river does not contain tench or carp, even though it may be slow flowing and have lots of reedy backwaters. The distribution of tench in rivers that suit them is mainly confined to East Anglia, and river carp are quite rare.

The grayling, which thrives in fast, clear rivers, where it vies for food with, and sometimes ousts the trout, is the often unwanted poor relation of the salmon family. This hardy fish, with the unmistakable 'sail-fin' dorsal, brings great joy to the coarse fisher's heart for it attains peak condition during the winter months, when it will feed avidly and give wonderful sport, despite frost, snow showers and freezing winds.

Small Streams and Brooks

It is the height of folly for any angler, no matter how experienced, to dismiss a small stream or brook with the idle thought, "Oh! I am sure there are no fish in there." I for one have been pleasantly surprised by the number and size of fish that can be seen in an apparently empty stream but one needs patience and often hours of watching from a concealed position to be able to locate them.

This type of small stream angling requires a very special approach. A most silent, roving technique is called for. The author takes a few fish here and there, usually in the deeper pools, and then moves on to another spot. Roach, dace, perch, grayling, pike, chub and occasionally rudd, may be present in these small stream fisheries. Quite often their size is amazing, especially when one considers the slight depth and width of the water from which they have been caught.

Canals, Drains and Dykes

Beginners to coarse fishing who have the good fortune to find themselves living in the midst of an area intersected by canals, drains and dykes, will discover a veritable wealth of angling waters at their disposal. Whilst lacking the purity, the power of flow, the wide assortment of fish and the picturesque beauty of rivers, these inland waterways and drainage system fisheries provide tens of thousands of coarse anglers with good sport and they can be an excellent training ground for the newcomer.

Don't expect to catch clear, fast water species of coarse fish—barbel, chub, grayling and dace—but be prepared for roach, perch, pike, eels, rudd and bream as well as for tench and a few carp.

One great drawback to most of these man-made fisheries is their open location and shallow depth. A lumbering, water's edge approach in broad daylight, would most certainly put every fish for miles around on the qui vive and ruin the angler's chances of sport for a considerable time. Stealth is the keyword when moving into position to begin fishing. The best approach to the desired spot is not along the bank but in a right angle direction from the surrounding fields or grassland—provided they contain no crops!

As with most coarse fishing, an early morning or late evening session will give the best results on canals, drains or dykes, the exceptions being the heavy, overcast days in summer and those dark, dismal ones in winter, when it hardly gets light from dawn to dusk.

Ponds and Lakes

Certain ponds and lakes, particularly those which are reed fringed and overhung with trees, have a wonderful 'fishy' appearance that instantly stirs the imagination when you first visit them. This type of water is apt to have a strong, captivating effect on some anglers so that they find themselves spending the whole of their leisure time just fishing and enjoying the quiet atmosphere.

They range from the smallest village pond, which could contain nothing but a few sticklebacks and eels, or conversely harbour a shoal of beautifully conditioned pound roach, to the largest of waters, per-haps over a hundred acres in size, full of monster carp, pike and tench.

Ponds and lakes, in all their varied depths, locations and sizes provide some of the most enjoyable fishing imaginable. Small ponds are apt to yield great surprises. Never underestimate their fish holding potential or write them off as useless before you have given them a thorough trial. Most often your catch will consist of just a few stunted roach and perch, with the odd large eel to bring a little hilarity to your sport, but occasionally you may find a shoal of fine, fat, rollicking tench, hitherto completely unsuspected by everyone living in the immediate vicinity.

To the angling beginner, small ponds with good fish stocks are an excellent morale booster. On a vast, deep water, the poor newcomer is liable to be a little bewildered and wonder where on earth to start fishing. The small water (I mean football pitch size) solves his problems. If he knows what sort of fish it contains, and has seen other anglers catching them in goodly numbers, he is reassured by the fact that wherever he sits he can't be very far away from his quarry. Generally, all the coarse fish, except the running water species—barbel, chub, dace and grayling—may be found to inhabit lakes and ponds. Due to the tremendous strides made in fishery management, coarse fish breeding and the importation of fish stocks from the Continent in recent years, carp have been placed in a great many still waters and are now being caught in ever increasing numbers and sizes.

Since ponds and lakes do not suffer the upsets of both dry and wet weather to the same extent as rivers, they can usually be relied upon to give more consistent fishing during the middle months of the year. However, some of them do have their sudden, disconcerting winter moods. They go 'dead' from the end of September until about the beginning of March. I have yet to find an acceptable explanation or cause for the apparent disappearance of the fish. One day they are all there, swimming around, splashing on the surface and being caught. A week later, when another visit is made, nothing can be seen or taken. When this is the case, the mid-winter period of three or four months must be allowed to elapse before the water comes back to life.

It is not usual to find a well-balanced variety of still water coarse fish in ponds or lakes, except where some attempt at proper fishery management has been undertaken by an interested owner, a fishing syndicate or a club renting the water.

Lots of ponds and lakes are disappointingly full of pygmy roach and perch, with a few very large eels feeding happily on them and attaining a great size. Such waters would not interest an angler of long standing but they can provide the beginner with the initial thrill of fish catching and give him that much needed first flush of angling confidence.

Gravel Pits

As the population explosion continues and more and more gravel and sand is quarried from the ground to build cities and to house the rapidly increasing number of people, gravel-pit fisheries will become vitally important if we are to afford a reasonable amount of angling facilities to everyone who is interested in coarse fishing.

Gravel pits, when matured can be stocked by natural methods, which takes a long time, or artificially, which is much quicker. They are extra special angling waters and have problems and characteristics peculiar only to themselves.

Before the modern ideas of landscaping the banks took hold, most gravel pits were left to fill with water and mature in their original state —with very precipitous, rough perimeters. This has proved both a boon and a hazard. To negotiate such banks in wet weather with your arms full of fishing tackle is a great feat of gymnastic ability. However, such places are very sheltered and afford the astute coarse fisher a chance to get well down at the edge of the water, below the wind level, and fish in comfort. To obtain the maximum advantage of this shelter, it is wise to go round the waters and map out their exact position with the aid of a compass, so that when those wintery winds do blow, a secluded wind-free fishing location can quickly be decided upon.

The depth of the water in some gravel pits is almost unbelievable and can cause quite a few angling complications. One very steep-banked pit which I saw in a pumped-out, dry state, resembled a huge bomb crater, fifty feet deep. Weed growth is usually limited to the perimeter only, and that is where the fish are to be found. On some gravel pits the accepted fishing style is to take up a position facing the wind, cast over the edge weeds and then allow the float tackle to drift back in, on to them. A long distance, far out into the middle casting style could prove most unproductive on some exceptionally deep waters for the bait is being cast into the very deep, cold 'desert' area of the centre part of the fishery—a place which is often completely devoid of all aquatic life! This method of fishing is best done with weighted leger tackle.

To fish gravel pits successfully it is usually best to see them before the gravel extraction work is finished. Then you can map them out roughly before they fill up with water. If on the other hand, they are established as fisheries, you can carefully work them over from the banks or, better still, plumb the depth from a boat which will give you a good idea of the underwater geography. This usually consists of a flat plateau, where the gravel ran out at a certain depth, and very deep holes when a good seam was struck. Unlike natural lakes and ponds, which are often quite regular in their water depth, gravel pits and brickponds can, and usually do, have a great water depth variation.

Large Lakes, Meres, Reservoirs and Non-Tidal Lochs

Huge, very deep waters quite often contain great shoals of outsize coarse fish, but unfortunately, the problem of locating them can be monumental. A boat is essential as marginal weed and reed growth precludes bank fishing in any form. On those vast stretches of open water where the surface area is more conveniently measured in square miles than acres, the vagaries of the weather must be taken into consideration at all times. In mountainous terrain, a strong wind funnelled in powerful gusts from a near-by valley, can whip up a three or four foot 'sea' which will rapidly swamp the ordinary style rowing boat. To bale with one hand and attempt to fish with the other, whilst keeping a wary eye on the weather, is definitely not conducive to enjoyable angling.

The present-day fashion of stocking new reservoirs with brown and rainbow trout does not meet with the approval of the water hungry coarse fisher who would prefer to see them made more suitable for his own kind of angling. However, I am quite certain that once the initial enthusiasm for game fishing has died down, a few of these waters, particularly those connected to rivers and streams, will be relegated to coarse fisheries by the people who control them. It usually happens that the coarse fish, which most persistently find their way into these reservoirs, breed so prolifically they overrun the trout and oust them out of existence.

In some Scottish lochs and Irish loughs, enormous pike are known to exist. Locating these huge fish is, to say the least, a difficult task, but to actually hook, play and successfully land or boat one is enormously satisfying to the coarse angler who has set his sights firmly on a record breaker. Only a few coarse anglers choose to tread such a lonely path. Most of us are usually quite satisfied to cast our lines into all kinds of waters, for any fish which may take our bait, and be eternally happy and grateful for the sport which they have given us.

CHAPTER 4

HOOKBAITS: METHODS OF FISHING
AND PRESENTATION

BEFORE I even begin to discuss coarse fishing baits and how to use them, I will hastily debunk certain preconceived ideas, harboured by most angling beginners, that magic or secret baits are used by expert anglers.

There is just no such thing as a deadly bait which will catch any species of coarse fish anytime, under all conditions of water and weather. Certain baits, at special times, when presented to the fish in the right manner, do seem to produce wonderful results: perhaps for a few days, weeks, a month, or even a whole season. However, just when the angler is deluding himself into thinking that he has made a fantastic angling discovery, the wonder bait starts to fail. Such angling lessons are most enlightening for they ensure that you become versatile in your bait selection and retain a sober, realistic attitude towards your knowledge of fish behaviour.

Worms

At the risk of being considered old-fashioned and a hopeless angling 'square', I will go on record and say that I have always had more faith in worms as an all round natural bait for any species of freshwater fish than anything else. What is more they can always be obtained free of charge, provided of course, you are prepared to do a little 'hands and knees' work on a lawn in the dark or wield a fork around the manure heaps.

'Free-lining' is a very simple, effective method of coarse fishing which few anglers ever get around to practising. They will everlastingly clutter up their line with bits and pieces which are quite unnecessary for certain angling circumstances. With just the rod, reel, line and baited hook, some most attractive methods of bait presentation can be made. In clear water, where the quarry can be plainly observed, a lively worm impaled once through the head on an appropriately sized hook can be cast and allowed to drift down to the bottom, or twitched in a sink and draw fashion.

This method will catch the largest and smallest of all the coarse fish. A great snake of a lobworm on a size 2 or 4 hook is suitable for carp, barbel, chub, pike and eels whilst a small redworm, mounted suitably on a size 12, 14 or 16 hook will take all the rest of the species. However,

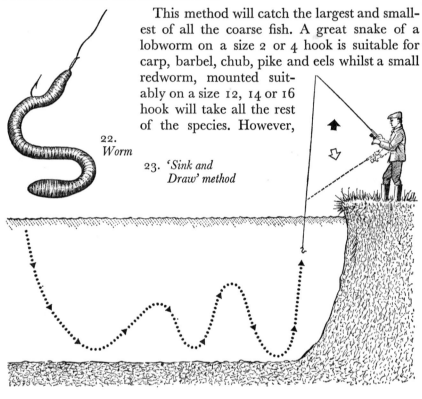

22.
Worm

23. *'Sink and Draw' method*

be prepared for sudden shocks at all times in angling. Your outsize worm offering may be taken by a two-pound roach whose mouth you fondly imagined would be quite incapable of engulfing such a hook. Perhaps, on the other hand, a tiny redworm with which you were attempting to lure a half-pound perch, will be suddenly seized by a yard long pike which will bend your light rod and pull your line taut past its breaking strain so that it snaps and falls slack.

Bread

Bread is another cheap hook offering which can be used in various forms to obtain different bait presentation effects. The modern 'assembly line', yeastless, steam-oven bread, with a thin, crisp crust and fluffy, 'cotton wool' middle is the stuff to use. Whilst I am sure such a chemical apology for the real thing plays havoc with the human digestion—I never eat it—coarse fish love it and devour it avidly. Always buy un-sliced loaves. The sliced variety, once it is taken from its waxed paper, usually dries out very quickly and is then only suitable for paste making or for use as 'crust'.

'Flake' is the new, fluffy inside crumb of the bread, roughly pinched off from the middle of the loaf. It can be moulded loosely around the hook with a small portion nipped firmly near the hook shank, to give holding bait retaining power. To facilitate casting, and to give the bait a little weight when fishing with the 'free-line' method, dunk the hook offering into the water for a second or two so that it becomes saturated, swells, and takes on an attractive shape. A suitable hook must be chosen to mount the 'flake' and this depends entirely on the size of the fish you are hoping to catch. Anything, from a size 2 or 4 with a bait of walnut dimensions will do for the large mouthed species, right down to a 16 or 18, with a tiny offering, for very fickle winter roach or dace.

24. Flake

Fresh bread crust, with some of the white crumb adhering, or stale crust cut into cubes

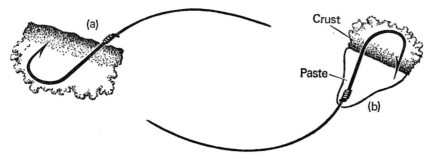

25. *Crust and Balanced Bread Bait.*

after being pressed between two boards overnight makes a wonderful 'free-line' bait.

The pressed stale crust is good for surface floating methods whilst the 'balanced', half crumb and half crust, or half crust and half paste bait, is first class for a slow sinking offering which will lie on the dense bottom weeds without becoming obscured.

Bread paste seems less popular with anglers these days, but I consider it an outstanding bottom-fished, float or leger-hook offering. Over gravel, sand, clay, firm mud or sparse weed, it will quite often take large roach, bream, rudd and tench although the quarry should be primed a few days before, or overnight with half a bucket of very well soaked mashed bread.

To make the basic paste, take out the white crumb middle from a stale loaf, place it in a clean cloth, and wet it thoroughly. Then, after squeezing out the surplus water by screwing the rag tight, knead it in the cloth until it is soft, malleable and of a smooth, lump-free texture. *It must be soft.* This is basic 'white breadpaste'. Colouring can be added, custard powder

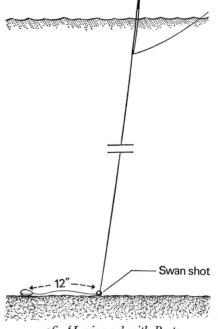

26. *'Laying on' with Paste.*

if you want it yellow, and aniseed oil if you fancy the smell and are sure the fish might do likewise.

The simplest and most pleasant way I know to fish still, deepish water with paste, is the 'rod in rest, tight line, bottom style'. Set up your tackle with a 7 or 8 in. quill float, attached by the bottom valve rubber only, then, to the end of the reel line, tie a size 10 or 12 spade-end hook. After plumbing the exact depth of your swim, slide the float up the line about a foot, towards the rod end, and nip on a swan shot at the same distance from the hook. It is immaterial if the shot is a little too heavy and sinks the float. We want the shot resting on the bottom and the bait with it, so if the shot is slightly overweight it doesn't really matter.

Bait up the hook by moulding a thumb-nail sized piece of paste around it, cast out carefully, allow the tackle to settle, then put the rod in the rests and gently tighten the line until the float just begins to be drawn towards you but is not pulled under. A quarter of an inch of the float tip is all that should show above the surface. If a fish mouths the bait and either lifts the shot or pulls it along the bottom, your delicately set float will indicate it clearly.

Maggots

Maggots are an easily obtained, convenient bait, sold at a price which will suit the pockets of everyone, provided of course, that they are not intended to be used as live groundbait and thrown in by the gallon, which would be rather expensive. Do not at this stage of your angling education become too deeply concerned and baffled by all the various types of maggots available, although there are three basic types which you should know; the hookbait maggots, either 'specials' nurtured on a bread and milk diet or 'gozzers' fed with poultry, game or pigeon flesh; feeders which are smaller maggots called 'pinkies' and 'squatts'and which are usually thrown into the water encased in groundbait balls; and of course the famed match fisher's special roach charmer, the 'caster', which is a very carefully produced and controlled maggot chrysalis.

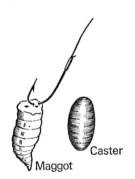

Caster

Maggot

When 'trotting the stream' on rivers for roach, maggots are the ideal bait and groundbait. A couple of pints (good tackle dealers always measure out the maggots in a pint measure and add the bran or sawdust later) will be sufficient for a three or four hour session, provided you are not too heavy handed with the free offerings.

In recent years the 'maggot saturation' method has been used by some Specimen Hunters. It certainly brings results in the way of fish catches, but unfortunately it is liable to produce a preoccupation phase, when

53

for a long time, the quarry go off all other hookbaits and become interested only in maggots.

Various other baits

There are other exotic and 'off beat' baits which can be offered to coarse fish and these are both legion in number and amazing in variety. I am quite certain that every coarse fisher, at some time or other, goes through a period when he becomes obsessed with constantly searching for, finding, and endlessly ringing the changes with his bait. Eventually he will reach the stage when he will use just a few tried and trusted baits although an exceedingly wide selection can be called upon when special circumstances warrant it.

Try to master the use of the three well tried and tested baits I have listed. Catch some fish on any of these, then, to gain greater experience, set out to take certain fish of your choice on a bait which you think they will accept. Eventually, you will reach the stage when you locate the fish first and then present them with an appropriate bait, rather than blindly trying a whole assortment of hook offerings in the fond hope that there may be some species of coarse fish in the water which will be prepared to feed on one of them.

Groundbait

I think this word was specially coined for anglers and that it must have a dual purpose. Used to define 'ground up bait', it aptly describes the fine, dry, bread-crumb mixture which, when wetted, is the most popular fish attractor used in coarse angling today. The 'ground' part of the word, I am sure, is also intended to indicate where the bait should be deposited: over the ground or bottom where the fish are expected to swim, feed upon it, and be caught.

In your close scrutinizing of the Angling press advertisement columns which I earlier recommended, you will have seen groundbait listed by suppliers and tackle dealers as 'Pure Ground White Bread'—'Coarse, Medium and Fine'. It can be bought by the pound, stone, or hundred-weight, according to your personal requirements.

Although this bread mixture (it is actually dried white bread ground up in large industrial grinders) is used by about seventy-five per cent of coarse fish anglers, there are, as with hookbaits, many other types of groundbait, each of which has its dedicated devotees. Fine bran and maize meal was one of the very earliest concoctions I used in my boyhood days. Horse manure, with lots of worms in it has proved a wonderful attractor for bream. Some devoted bream and tench fishermen actually fill a large tin bath at the waterside with a dozen or so stale loaves, thoroughly wet them and then mash them to a gooey pulp to obtain the right mixture.

The golden rule for groundbaiting is to use a solid, stiff mixture for fast flowing, deep rivers and a loose, crumbly one for shallow, still water. The modern polythene washing-up bowl is an ideal receptacle for mixing 3 or 4 lbs. of groundbait. Always add the water to the groundbait. Put in a small amount at a time, taking care to have a good amount of dry groundbait left on hand to 'dry off' a mix should you go a little wild with the use of the water and swamp the groundbait that is being prepared.

Two distinct types of groundbaiting are commonly practised. Prebaiting which is the introduction of regular quantities of feed on each of several days *before* fishing commences, and the groundbaiting which takes place during the time when the angler is fishing.

The first kind can be very effective just before the Open Season commences, when the chosen swim has been reasonably well cleared of obstructions or dense weed and the fish are congregated by free food at twenty-four hourly intervals. This type of pre-feeding campaign gives good results, provided the water is fairly secluded or private. Nothing can be more infuriating than to discover at dawn on Open Season day, that your pitch is already occupied by a strange angler pulling out fish to his heart's content, and that it is your groundbait which is bringing him his unusual success!

Live and Dead Fish as Baits

Until just a couple of decades ago, only a few of the coarse fish species were considered to have predominant or part-time predatory habits and instincts. However, experiments in recent years, by advanced anglers have revealed that all of them do, at times, devour their own kind, both dead and alive.

Small live fish, lightly hooked through the bottom or top lip and allowed to swim by the 'free-line' method, are a deadly bait for almost any hungry coarse fish at certain times of the season. Barbel particularly, are fond of a live fish menu in the first month or so of the coarse fish season, around late June and early July. That inveterate live fish devourer and freshwater shark, the pike, can be relied upon to attack anything that moves be it fish, flesh or fowl, when it is on the rampage and feeling hungry. Perch and chub love chasing minnows in the shallows and will therefore strike fiercely at small livebaits, spinners and plugs which are worked in the vicinity of reed clumps or over weedbeds.

Another recent innovation which has confounded the theories of the early angling sages, is the static, bottom-fished deadbait. Without exception, the original pike experts wrote of the pike lying deep in the water and attacking its prey as it passed overhead. That a pike might pick up a meal as it foraged on the bottom did not occur to many anglers until a few bold-thinking innovators tried the 'deadbait' method and found it would work and take the biggest of pike on days when they were very dour and not inclined to chase after their prey. As further proof that anglers were becoming less hidebound, two saltwater deadbaits, herrings and sprats, were used and found effective. These eliminated the great snag which had previously arisen when small roach, perch or rudd for deadbait could not be caught in very hard, wintery weather.

The question of using live fish for baits has lately brought about a great ethical controversy. Whilst some anglers have no qualms about impaling a lively minnow on a hook for bait, they would consider the use of a half-pound roach unthinkable. At the other end of the scale, are avid pike fishers who most seriously and without inhibitions use very large livebaits—2 or 3 lb. bream and even 'jack' pike in the 3 to 5 lb. weight range—to catch monster pike which could not be tempted by smaller offerings.

Each angler must decide for himself how he feels about this branch of coarse fishing and steadfastly pursue his own chosen path. The modern trend is away from livebaiting, but there are top class pike catchers who still pin their faith on nothing but live-fish baits. Their catches of pike in the very high weight bracket would seem to prove that their consistent success is due to their adherence to what is rapidly being thought of as a very archaic and cruel baiting method.

Spinners, Plugs and Lures

The coarse fishing beginner who is making his first approach to angling at the present time is entering the field just when the tackle and other equipment for 'sportfishing', as the world of artificial baiting is called, is reaching a state of high efficiency. From all over the world—America, Sweden, France, Japan, Germany and Norway—rods, reels and most important, wonderful lures, are being imported and put on to the tackle market.

Special, slightly shorter, more powerful rods are used for this type of angling and also for both live and deadbaiting when heavy baits have to be cast. These baits necessitate a higher breaking strain line, something around the 10 lb. mark. You will find these rods described as

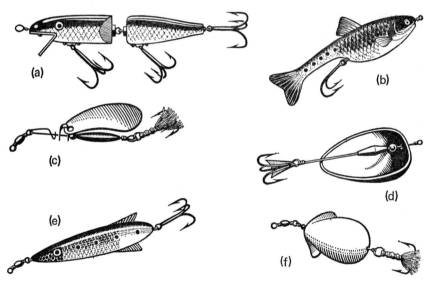

28. *A selection of Artificial Lures.*
(a) Double jointed plug   (b) Soft-rubber or plastic fish
(c) Kidney spoon   (d) Vibro spoon
(e) Large 'toby'   (f) 'Colorado' spoon.

'Pike and Spinning Rods'. They are invariably two piece, and range from 7 to about 10 ft. in length.

Pike are the main target for this roving, all action category of coarse fishing, but perch often surprise pike anglers by hotly pursuing and taking large artificial lures which would be considered too big for their smaller mouths. The attraction of 'sportfishing' from a boat powered by an outboard motor is very great, as a huge expanse of water can be given a very thorough working over which would be utterly impossible for the angler operating from the bank.

The lures for this fishing are many and varied and I have seen expert anglers lugging around great cantilever shelved boxes which contain two or three hundred different types. Some of the prices asked for the top grade American imported lures are breathtaking—so high that the ordinary angler would shrink from casting one into a snaggy spot for fear of losing it.

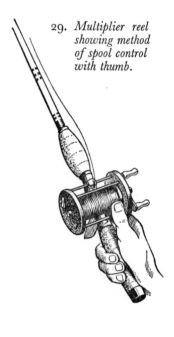

29. *Multiplier reel showing method of spool control with thumb.*

We can divide the whole range of artificial baits into three categories: the old-fashioned, traditional spinners or spoons, which as their name implies, revolve when they are drawn through the water; wobblers which are wood or plastic and do not spin, but sway from side to side in a sinuous manner; and last, and very much in vogue these days, the lures which have special antics, like diving, floating, popping, surface skittering and even jumping right out of the water! Most of these effects are produced by the incorporation of metal vanes, set at very exact angles to produce realistic, lifelike effects which simulate all the panic stricken ditherings of a fish, a reptile or a small animal in distress.

For this angling, where constant, often very long casts are being made, the fixed-spool reel beats the centre-pin hands down. One other type of reel, the multiplier, must now be considered, as it is most effective and popular for lure fishing. The multiplier reel, as its name suggests, is a geared reel on the lines pin reel, but many more For instance, the very wide, light and of a revolving drum centre-refinements have been added. drum which holds the line is revolves freely in a 'cage' when the 'free spool' mechanism is engaged. Good quality multi-plier reels for this kind of fishing are expensive but a joy to use when they have been thoroughly mastered. The mechanical aids with which they are fitted make casting, retrieving and playing a good fish, the greatest of angling pleasure.

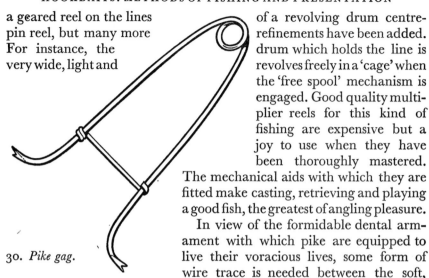

30. *Pike gag.*

In view of the formidable dental arm-ament with which pike are equipped to live their voracious lives, some form of wire trace is needed between the soft, easily severed nylon line and the lure, which often disappears well back into the long, crocodilian maw of this fish. There are two kinds of trace wire in general use: single-strand steel wire, which is fairly stiff and prone to kinking, and a softer, twisted, multi-strand wire which can be obtained with or without nylon covering. To avoid line twist when spinning baits are used, and also to facilitate the quick changing of lures, various types of swivels can be incorporated into the terminal trace tackle.

One should again stress the need for the utmost care when landing, unhooking or returning pike. Their teeth are not only sharp pointed, *they are also razor edged*. A set of hook extracting tools is very necessary for this job and they should comprise two or three different sized gags for holding the jaws firmly apart and at least two pairs of very long handled forceps. One false move anywhere near the teeth of a pike with your finger ends and a severe gashing will occur, even if the skin is just lightly brushed by them!

CHAPTER 5

THE FISH

IT is not my intention, in this lengthy chapter which will deal with a dozen different species, to parade before the inexperienced angler a long list of all the record coarse fish, their captors, weights and waters where taken. Such a welter of facts and figures would make very dry reading to a beginner who may not even have wet a line. In any case, records are liable to be broken, or established ones abandoned in the light of fresh evidence, which perhaps casts a grave doubt upon their authenticity.

I will begin by listing the species of coarse fish which the beginner can expect to take with a limited amount of fairly simple, inexpensive tackle on almost any near-by water. Towards the end of the chapter, I will list the more difficult, larger species which require a specialized approach and tackle.

It is a grave error to fish at all times with a deadly serious, unwavering, concentration and only be satisfied when the largest possible fish has been safely netted. By pursuing such a soul destroying course you may be able to boast a great number of weighty captures, but these will be a disappointing reward when you compare them with all the other delightful fish you might have caught had you brought your sights down to a more reasonable level.

As a very rough guide, known maximum growth weights will be given, but when these are halved, they generally represent the largest size of that particular species of fish which anglers are most likely to encounter during normal fishing sessions. Be satisfied with such a top weight target for the time being until you become thoroughly proficient on all waters, with all types of fish; then, after a while you can allow yourself to soberly contemplate the dizzy heights of record weight fishing.

31 *(right). Float tackle for still water roach fishing.*

Roach

The roach qualifies for the title 'The Coarse Fisher's Bread and Butter Fish' as it is usually the very first one which the amateur angler encounters and succeeds in catching. At times it has been confused with the rudd, the dace, and even small chub. Until you become adept at fish identification, look for an upper jaw which protrudes slightly over the lower one and a dorsal fin which is set slightly more forward than that of the rudd.

River and still water roach love and thrive in clean water that has a gravel or sand bottom. The biggest grow to a weight of about 4 lbs. Bearing in mind my observations on the weight aspect, expect to catch a 2 lb. roach only in the most exceptional circumstances, and one in excess of that magical figure, only in your wildest dreams!

The lightest of tackle can be used for the general run-of-the-mill roach, which will be found in goodly numbers in most waters. They will usually be very prolific in the 3 or 4 oz. weight range and gradually become less numerous as they move up the weight scale to the lb. mark. Over that, they can be classed as 'big roach'. You will need a lot of skill and effort before you are able to take them regularly.

In still waters during the summer months, a bait fished on or near the bottom, either before the sun has started to rise too high or after it has dipped well down, will usually take the best sample of fish that are in the water. The whole tackle set-up must be light, well balanced and in no way coarse or clumsy. A light match fisher's rod in the 12 ft. range is ideal. The reel should be a fixed-spool if long casting is desired, or a centre-pin if the margins are being fished. You can have the line strength as low as you like, even down to a 1 lb. breaking strain if the fish are very shy and only small. Likewise, use a light quill or balsa bodied cane-stemmed float and just enough shot, spaced at regular intervals along the line, to enable you to cast the tackle with the minimum water disturbance.

When using a maggot hookbait, 'loose feed' maggots can be thrown in at intervals, perhaps every fourth cast, so that they actually scatter around the area where the float and terminal tackle have settled.

The very height of angling pleasure can be attained when fishing for roach if the angler can visit a first-class river at the time of season and when the state of water is most appropriate for 'trotting the stream'. Autumn, and often spells in mid-winter, produce the right weather when the days are unexpectedly mild and the water level is neither too high and floody, or low and clear.

Slightly heavier tackle will be needed for this running water fishing and the rod needs to be of the 'Avon' style. It is ideally operated in conjunction with a good centre-pin reel, a 2 or 3 lb. line, a cork jacketed float carrying 3 or 4 medium shot, and a hook size according to the baits mentioned for still water.

A nice, streamy, straightish run, free from obstructions, is the place to look for. Fish the bait so that it just trundles along clear of the bottom, or above any weeds, and 'feed' the 'float path' with offerings of maggots, chopped worms or well damped mashed bread. This will get the roach swimming upstream against the current towards you.

Perhaps you will commence your fishing career on a very easy roach water and take quite a few sizeable ones without a great deal of trouble. Even so, never underestimate the roach. Whatever stage of angling proficiency you may reach you will never fail to be surprised how difficult it is to catch very big roach regularly.

Perch

The perch is quite unmistakable and a great joy to all those young boys who fish with great worms impaled on outsize hooks. With their high, spikey dorsal fin, perpendicular black bars and capacious bony mouth they cannot possibly be confused with any other species except perhaps, the ruffe, and only then when both fish are very small.

Tiny perch gladden the hearts of angling beginners by voraciously

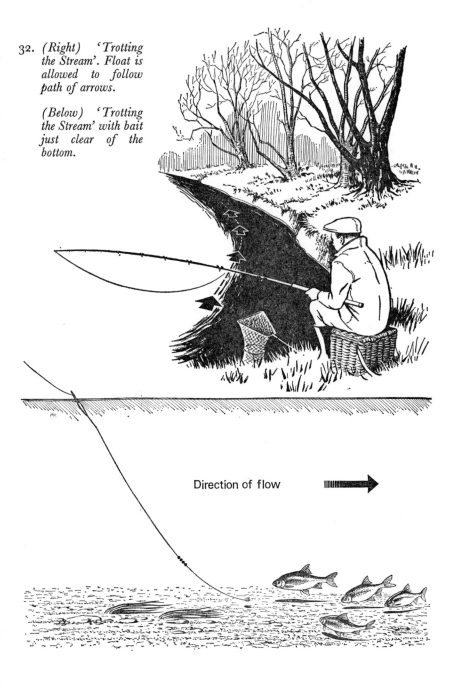

32. *(Right)* *'Trotting the Stream'. Float is allowed to follow path of arrows.*

(Below) *'Trotting the Stream' with bait just clear of the bottom.*

Direction of flow

gobbling up worm and maggot baits and absolutely refusing not to be hooked; usually they take the bait far down into their innards. On the other hand, big perch, those in the 3 or 4 lb. weight category, are extraordinarily difficult to catch. I know of no angler who specializes in, and is regularly successful with big perch catching. Plenty of fishermen concentrate on angling for them, but they are such enigmatic fish that very few are taken, and those that are usually come to the landing net when they are least expected.

Perch reach a top weight of about 6 lbs. but as stated earlier, one half of that weight is a very fine fish indeed—a rare catch to be proud of. I can think of no other fish which will better set the angling beginner on fire with enthusiasm than this one. They are widely distributed in most waters, both still and flowing, but appear to grow largest in deep gravel pits and lakes where an abundance of small fish are present to afford them a rich, growth making diet.

Lobworms, on large hooks, size 2, 4 or 6 are a fine big perch bait, so also are small, bright scaled live fish, hooked lightly through the lip and 'free-lined' or fished below a float which will only just support them. Buoy type bung floats should be avoided as they not only give great resistance to a taking fish but prove a handicap if they have to be drawn back through reed or weedbeds.

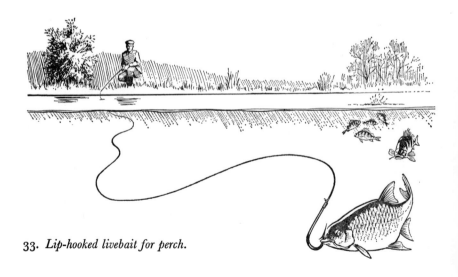

33. *Lip-hooked livebait for perch.*

In very large, still waters, where just a few outsize perch are known to be present, a 'far off' legering technique is frequently the only method that will produce any sort of results. If two rods are employed for this 'sit back and await results' brand of fishing, different baits can be tried, the two most reliable being outsize lobworms and small dead fish. Avoid the use of a casting weight which is too heavy. The biting fish, if they are at all finicky, will be most suspicious of moving off with a bait which gives a very heavy unnatural amount of resistance.

Complicated terminal rigs should be disdained for all forms of coarse fishing unless they have been proved to take fish with astounding regularity. Where long casting is necessary, with baits which are too light to provide enough weight in themselves, a small Arlesey bomb in the $\frac{1}{8}$ to $\frac{1}{2}$ oz. range, can be slotted on the reel line through its swivel. It can be stopped from sliding down towards the hook, which is tied below it, by means of a split shot nipped on the line.

In view of the fact that perch of all sizes are very active, predatory fish, they will respond well to all forms of spinning, lure fishing tactics. Very large perch will sometimes follow, attack and take outsize pike spinners but generally speaking, small, bright spinners and lures take perch most effectively. These should on no account be jerked out of the water at the end of the retrieve whilst they are still a rod's length from the bank. Quite often, in clear deeply shelved lakes, a large perch will be seen following the spinner right into the bank but turning aside at the last moment as the subject of its interest is lifted out from under its very nose. When this occurs, try two dodges either of which may result in the fish being caught.

Firstly, speed up the lure with a fast jerk just before the end of the spin. This may bring a rapid acceleration from the fish and a plunge on the rod top that is so strong it almost tears it from your grasp. Alternatively, as soon as the spinner comes into sight, with attendant perch, stop reeling in and allow it to cease its movement through the water and flutter in a dead fashion down to the bottom. Next, and this is most important, leave it there for a few minutes. Against all the accepted rules of angling and to your complete amazement, the perch may actually pause over the stationary spinner, inspect it, and then suddenly swallow the lot in a flash!

In all types of angling there can never be any rigid, inflexible rules, only a few very loose ones. What is more, you don't make them, the fish do, and they break them again a short time later. At first this will be very mystifying, but eventually, as you progress along the road to piscatorial knowledge, you will even be enlightened by your failures and filled with eager anticipation for the next unexpected occurrence in fish behaviour.

Bream

This is one fish with which anglers have either a love or hate relationship, according to the branch of coarse fishing which they follow. Match fishermen welcome bream into their swim because if they are present in goodly numbers and intent on feeding, the angler can easily fill a keep net and be among the winners at weigh-in time.

Angling beginners will find the bream very obliging and also a great morale booster for their slab-sided shape makes even the pounders look impressively large. In addition, bream of that size usually give a long, slow, steady bite indication, with much float dithering. This endearing habit allows anyone whose angling reflexes are not fully sharpened to have plenty of time to hook them.

There are two distinct species of bream; the silver and the common or bronze bream. The former variety can be loosely referred to as the 'lesser' bream as few are known to have been taken much above the 2½ lb. mark, but the bronze bream must decidedly qualify for the title 'greater' as it is known to exceed 13 lbs. and estimated by reliable, knowledgeable anglers to attain weights well in excess of that, even up to 15 or 16 lbs.

The anglers who loathe and detest bream and go to any lengths to avoid catching them, are invariably big carp and tench fishermen. These fishermen often spend weeks clearing weed from a productive looking patch of water only to find, after pre-baiting it with a choice selection of groundbait, that the place is alive with bottom-browsing bream, all around the 2 lb. mark. They consider this quarry not worthy of such a sustained effort and certainly not one which they expect to find dining sumptuously off the free banquet they had intended a more delectable species to enjoy.

Look for bream in slow flowing muddy drains or rivers, and in ponds, lakes, canals and gravel pits. This is the one fish of which the inexperienced angler can make a great catch, should he be so fortunate as to locate a vast shoal in a serious feeding mood.

Nothing very special in the way of tackle or angling method is required for those bream which run up to a weight of 3 or 4 lbs. They are hardly spirited fighters and an ordinary hollow glass 12 ft. match rod with a line of 2 or 3 lbs. breaking strain will land them, provided they are taken in snag free water.

Float watching, rather than the somewhat 'blank wall' staring at either a rod tip or bite indicator when legering, seems to be the more eye-pleasing method of catching coarse fish, so by all means give yourself the pleasure of float fishing for bream whenever the depth of water is suitable.

The bait should be presented on or near the bottom where the bream will be avidly tucking into the mashed bread, chopped worms or maggots which you should have put in either the previous day or at the commencement of the fishing session. Have plenty of the same groundbait in reserve in order to regularly feed the shoal and stop them wandering off.

Big bream—those in excess of 6 or 7 lbs.—are definitely not a beginner's fish. On odd occasions, they are taken unintentionally by anglers who are not fishing exclusively for them: but only a few 'specialists' take big bream regulary by design. The whole trouble with shoal fish—and the bream is one of these—is that the shoals are not made up of different sized fish ranging from very small to very large, but rather of fish of the same size. Very big shoals are usually made up of the smallest fish, whilst the real whoppers seem to swim in the select company of just two or three other fish of a similar size.

It is quite safe to fish for bream in the lower weight category with a light rod, 3 lb. line and a size 14 or 16 hook. However, if you really intend having a serious, concentrated early morning, late evening or all night session with the larger ones, you will need to scale up your tackle strength a good deal. Use a more powerful, 'capable' rod, 5 or 6 lb. line and thicker wired hooks in the 10, 12 or 14 size range. Never forget, that although you may be able to hook a big fish easily on a small, fine hook you will not be able to hold or land it on such a weak link in your tackle.

Rudd

I am a little uncertain why such a handsome fish as the rudd is not more popular with anglers. Perhaps the fact that it is not so widely distributed in our coarse fishing waters as other species has some bearing on the matter. Dare I suggest that many anglers take rudd regularly but fail to identify them correctly as such and group them in with their roach catches?

As the rudd reputedly feeds on or near the surface, it is equipped by nature with a bottom lip which overlaps the top one. However, this mouth position theory should not be taken too seriously; at times, all the coarse fish will be found to feed both on the top and at the bottom. Artificial flies, fished on the surface have been taken by all the species, including eels! Conversely, baits legered on the bottom have also accounted for all the so-called surface feeders.

But to return to the rudd and how to identify it. Generally, its body shape will be found to be deeper and heavier than that of the roach. As its name implies, it seems to glow with redness in sunlight and be suffused with a deep golden sheen when viewed in the evening by the light of the setting sun. An imaginary line, drawn vertically from the back edge of the dorsal fin, will just about connect with the front of the anal fin. In the roach, the dorsal fin is further forward, approximately above the pelvic or ventral fins.

Rudd are fish of the reedy margins and weedbeds. They grow to a bigger size than the roach, about $4\frac{1}{2}$ lbs., but forget that weight if you want to enjoy your angling to the fullest extent. Think, instead, of a 2 lb. rudd as a wonderful capture, which believe me, it really is.

The general purpose, coarse fishing tackle which is suitable for roach is also ideal for rudd, but do bear in mind the snag factor when fishing for rudd among dense reeds and bankside tangles on overgrown river backwaters, canals, lakes or meres. The line strength should be stepped up to at least 4 or 5 lb. breaking strain, not to beat the fish, but as a safeguard against continual tackle losses through the hook or float becoming caught up in the 'jungle'.

Maggot chrysalis, or in modern angling jargon, the 'caster', is a wonderful bait for rudd. Even if the fish are not showing on the surface, it is possible to induce them to feed madly with free offerings of this bait.

Warm, thundery evenings are the best. If a brilliant orange sunset follows the heavy rain showers of the day then the conditions are perfect. A good handful of chrysalis should be thrown in to start the proceedings, then the angler should sit quietly and await the surface activity which will surely follow.

A few dimpling rises will appear here and there and gradually the whole area will be alive with feeding rudd. The line for this type of fishing must be fairly light and fine. $1\frac{1}{2}$ or 2 lbs. is ideal. Use a smallish 'toothpick' porcupine float secured with valve rubbers top and bottom, just one small shot right underneath it and a fine wired size 16 hook, which will neatly pierce the caster without splitting it badly and opening it up.

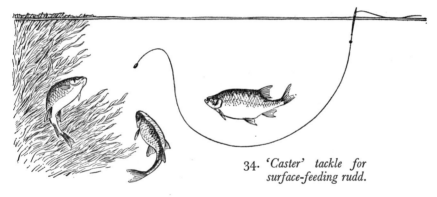

34. 'Caster' tackle for surface-feeding rudd.

In placing the lead shot right below the float, a slow sinking bait effect is achieved. By setting the float about 3 or 4 ft. above the hook, the action by the angler can be almost continuous. The fish should take the caster bait 'on the drop' whilst it is slowly sinking to its lowest point. The tackle is retrieved every twenty or thirty seconds. A few more free offerings are thrown in to keep the fish actively feeding, then a fresh cast is made.

Bread flake and surface fished crust are two other deadly rudd baits. Hungry rudd can be induced to feed avidly on the surface by scattering quarter slices from a thin cut loaf and allowing them to drift right into the reedbeds, where a great splashing and rustling will be heard as the rudd go to work, tearing apart and sucking down the floating feed. As stated earlier in this chapter, a stronger line must be used for this angling and a snag proof type of terminal tackle must be arranged. The float is the offending article that usually jams in the reedstems, so to ensure that it makes a free passage through them, mount it on the line with two long pieces of valve rubber which project well beyond both ends.

For this kind of angling, where tackle losses are expected, the advantages of 'tied direct' hooks will be appreciated. With a 'spade-end' hook or an eyed one, tied direct to the reel line with one of the knots illustrated, it is a simple matter to pull free 'for a break' should the hook become stuck fast. If it is lost (the line invariably breaks at the knot) merely tie on a fresh hook from the tackle box and continue fishing. When shop bought hooks to yard long nylon links are used, the whole tackle set-up has to be renewed. This is time consuming and infuriating, especially if all around you the fish are feeding madly and recklessly devouring your free feeds.

Tench

Of all the coarse fish species, the tench is by tradition the one which anglers seek in the early, misty morning on the first day of the Open Season.

It is essentially a summer fish and the period of its activity lasts from about the beginning of June until very early Autumn. Coarse fishing beginners will have not the slightest difficulty in recognizing it when they manage to land their first one. Power is apparent in every detail of its body and fin shape. From its great square edged, spatulate tail and its broad, powerful, paddle shaped anal, dorsal, pelvic and pectoral fins to its thick, rounded shoulders, it is a formidable opponent to have on the end of a line—and heaven help you if your tackle is unsound!

The colouring of tench varies in different waters. At times they are almost an overall black with startling red eyes, shining like rubies in a sea of jet. On other occasions, when they are found in deep, weedy pools, they will be dark green or golden in colour. In gravel pits they may be pale fawn. I can call to mind one deep gravel pit which holds a head of the palest fawn tench I have ever seen, almost albino in colouring.

Tench grow to about 8 or 9 lbs. but 'specimens' are deemed to weigh around 5 lbs. A fish that size will tax both the angling ability and tackle of anyone who succeeds in hooking it, especially if it has to be played and landed amidst snags or in the vicinity of thick weedbeds. They are lovers of sluggish, muddy rivers, canals or drains and grow to their greatest attainable size in sheltered, soft-bottomed ponds and lakes which have abundant weed growth and a rich, ever present larder of teeming aquatic life.

Ordinary coarse fishing tackle will serve for the smaller tench up to about 3 lbs. Over that weight, especially in weedy waters, it is a folly to attempt serious tench fishing for the 4, 5 and 6 pounders without a good resilient 'Avon' rod, a 5 or 6 lb. line and an assortment of strong, correctly tempered spade-end or eyed hooks ranging from size 2 down to about 14.

Swim or pitch preparation has long been considered a vital part of tench fishing by the serious minded big fish addicts. Personally, I feel that it is overdone at times as too much water and bank disturbance can upset the fishing, especially if whole gangs of anglers concentrate upon preparing dozens of pitches by ruthlessly tearing out great gaping holes in the weedbeds and then dumping in endless buckets of groundbait.

35.
Float at 'half-cock'

The widely accepted method of fishing for tench is with the bait firmly anchored to the bottom by one or two large shot and a quill float set at the exact water depth so that it just leans at 'half-cock' when it is attached to the line by its bottom ring or rubber valve tube sleeve.

In theory, the moment the fish picks up the bait the float should rise up in the water, fall over and lay flat, before streaking off or bobbing gently away according to the mood of the taking fish. On many occasions this is exactly what happens and the tench which give these copy book bites are easily hooked. However, there are times when the fish seem very fickle. They tweak the end of your worm or maggot bait and nibble small pieces if you are using bread. The float twitches, dithers and slowly sways, but never dives under in the heart-stopping style which denotes a genuine, full-blooded tench bite. This is an infuriating problem which can happen with quite a few of the coarse fish species. Sometimes the answer is to scale down your tackle by using a finer line and smaller hooks so that the quarry overcome their shyness and give a bold, decisive bite.

Quite often these tactics prove effective and immediately after the line and hook have been changed a number of good fish will be taken. Eventually, the 'twitching' float indications will return but should a further scaling down of tackle have to be made it is usual to find that the strength of line and size of hook required to obtain bites and hook the fish are much too low in breaking strain and holding power to give the angler a ghost of a chance to land them.

Contrary to common angling theory, tench do not always feed on the bottom at dawn and dusk. Sometimes, in quite shallow water—about 3 or 4 ft. deep—they will sport around just under the surface in glaring midday sunshine and actually allow themselves to be taken in goodly numbers on single maggot baits mounted on small hooks fished at mid-water level.

The very biggest of the tench, the real monsters of, dare I say it, just under 10 lbs., certainly require some study and concentration. They are the devil's own job to locate, monumentally difficult to hook and a veritable impossibility to land. I am sorry to paint so black a picture but very few anglers have been successful with really large tench.

Dace

The dace, I am sure, is a fish which was sent by the Angler's Guardian Angel to give him unlimited sport in his initial stages. The smaller ones are easy to catch, and are to be found in most tiny brooks, streams and rivers in large shoals. They feed avidly during the hot, bright sunlit hours of the day when most other fish are lying doggo.

Very fine tackle can be used as the grandfathers of the dace species only weigh about 1½ lbs. and any angler regularly taking dace of 8 to 12 ozs. can consider himself very skilful. 'Trotting the stream' with light float tackle and a generous supply of maggots for both hookbait and groundbait is the most popular and pleasant method of taking good bags of dace. A light 12 ft. match rod, used in conjunction with a 2 lb.

line on the reel of your choice—fixed-spool or centre-pin—is the tackle which will handle any dace you are liable to encounter. Nothing fancy in floats is needed, just a medium-sized bird or porcupine quill which needs two or three evenly spaced shot to cock and settle it down in the water so that only a small amount of the tip shows above the surface.

Hooks need to be fine-wired and small, size 14, 16 or 18. The single maggot bait should be nicked through the skin on to the hook at the head, or wide end of the maggot.

Generally, dace do not take a great deal of locating, especially in summer. They will invariably be found in the fast flowing, shallow runs below weirs and where there is a shelving sand or gravel bottom with luxuriant growths of weed in close proximity. In winter, like the roach, they tend to move into deeper water that has a slower, steadier flow, but they can be relied upon to feed during daylight even when the most severe arctic weather conditions prevail.

High summer is of course the time of year when dace fishing is at its best. To be able to fish a first-class water where the dace are both prolific and run to a good average size, is an angling initiation which every fisherman in the making should try to experience quite early in his angling career.

On a nice straight 'glide' where the river runs steady and at an even depth, it is a wonderful tonic for the angler's morale if he is able to sit down with dace in mind and then a few minutes later begin catching those very same fish. They respond well to loose feed maggots. This term 'loose feed' can be taken to imply hookbait samples used as groundbait and distributed on the scatter principle. Another way of groundbaiting with maggots is to enclose a few in the middle of a groundbait ball made up of a bread, bran, cereal or other fish attracting mixture.

When a really good supply of maggots is readily available—and by that I mean a gallon at least—this loose feeding, with a handful being thrown in every ten minutes or so, will keep the dace interested and feeding steadily the whole day through. However, as maggots in such quantities are rather expensive, a couple of pints can be eked out if they are introduced into the swim by the groundbait-ball method already mentioned.

There is one most important point I must raise as regards this 'trotting the stream' or 'long-trotting' method of fishing running waters. The basic idea is that the angler sits at a fixed point on the riverbank and drops his specially arranged tackle into the water in front of him. He then allows it to be carried downstream by the current until such time as the float is no longer visible, the tackle reaches a snaggy area or the distance separating angler and float is so great that it would be impossible for him to strike and hook the fish. That is 'long trotting' under ideal conditions but there are many variations. Sometimes, on very bendy, snaggy, tree-lined waters, there may be only a few short stretches suitable for 'trotting'. This type of water is often more productive than a copybook, open banked one, as any form of vegetation close to the water will prove an added attraction to the fish. Try to be completely unmoved by the thoughts of tackle losses when faced with a very 'fishy' looking, but snag ridden swim. If you can 'trot' your tackle downstream, just five to ten yards, and hold it back right among the overhanging branches of a wicked thorn bush, do not be afraid to do so. You will most certainly misjudge your distance once or twice and lose a couple of floats and hooks, but the fish you could take in such a location will amply compensate you for your losses.

Chub

This is a fish which in its smaller sizes (up to the $1\frac{1}{2}$ lb. mark) can be, and often is, confused with the dace. Let us therefore immediately delve into the obvious identification details so that someone fresh and eager on the river, who sees himself as the new dace record holder, does not suddenly find he is actually a very ordinary, red-faced small chub captor!

The dorsal and the anal fins are the points to note. On the dace, the top edge of the dorsal fin is concave, so also is the back, or trailing edge of the anal fin. The same two fins on the chub are exactly opposite in shape. Both dorsal and anal on this fish are convex.

It will be noted also that as the chub becomes heavier and leaves the dace weight range behind, it gets much rounder, thicker and torpedo shaped; in fact 'chubbier' as its name implies. Quite a few breathtaking chub have been caught in the weight range of 7 to $8\frac{1}{2}$ lbs. in the last two decades and it appears that some Scottish salmon rivers hold chub in excess of 10 lbs. By taking that figure as the upper limit of the chub's growth potential, a five pounder is a magnificent fish.

Chub are essentially fish of lively, running water although they will not always be found in such a well oxygenated environment. They have been introduced by design—and infiltrated by accident—into certain still waters, gravel pits, canals and lakes. Their progress in such fisheries has been quite unpredictable and some surprising results have occurred. Occasionally, in waters which have a rich amount of natural food, a prolific weed growth and most important, some underwater effervescence or seepage, they have thrived, bred, and grown to a weighty, hard-fighting size. But in water conditions that are all wrong, they just hang

36. *Anal Fin Comparison.*
(a) Chub   (b) Dace.

on to life grimly, turn cannibal, develop large heads and emaciated bodies, and eventually expire.

'Trotting the stream' is a sound method which will seldom fail to take good catches of small and average-sized chub. The tackle must be, to quote a favourite term of mine, 'quite adequate'. By that I mean sound in every item and able to land the biggest chub which your imagination can conjure up. If it is not, then—bang—a fish will take your bait and smash you up with ease.

A long 'Avon' style rod is the one to use on open, fairly snag-free waters. The line strength for the angler's peace of mind should be around 5 or 6 lb. breaking strain. The big baits which the outsize mouthed chub can comfortably gulp down will necessitate a 'tied direct' to reel line hook, of around size 10, 8, 6 or 4, according to what is mounted on it. To support these quite large offerings, floats will need to be larger and they in turn require more lead shot to cock them and make them ride the water correctly with just an easily seen tip visible. Good big chunks of bread, crust, lobworms or bunches of maggots will usually take the fish which are not fussy feeders, but to add a little finesse, raid the cheese platter before you embark on a chub fishing outing and try them with any sort you can lay your hands upon.

Preferably give them something which is inclined to be soft and round, rather than hard and sharp cornered. Mould the cheese round the hook and conceal the whole of it, eye or spade-end included, but leave the point just 'peeping' to avoid it being 'blanketed' by the bait when a strike is made.

37. *Cheese on hook with point just peeping out.*

'Free lining'—when just a baited hook at the end of the reel line is employed —can be the most effective all-round chub catching method. It enables all depths of water and even the most snag ridden 'jungles' to be worked without time-consuming tackle adjustment. Live minnows, small frogs, big black slugs (handle them with old sugar tongs) and all manner of live, natural offerings can be used.

Very big chub, those crafty tree root and undercut bank-loving giants of 5 lbs. and above, require a special 'jungle patrol' technique if you are ever to locate, stalk and finally grass them. They are to be found in heavily-bushed, tree-lined, overgrown stretches of rivers and streams.

For this type of 'poke and dangle' fishing, which is commonly known in angling parlance as 'dapping', a short, resilient rod is needed, a sound centre-pin reel, some 7 or 8 lb. line, and a good supply of strong, sharp hooks in all the larger sizes. The general idea is to spot the fish first, try to work your way noiselessly into a position to offer it a bait, and then 'play it by ear' from that point on. Often you will dangle the bait near a fair-sized chub only to see something twice its size shoot up from the depths, take the offering with a tackle breaking crash and disappear again leaving you shattered and trembling.

If you are legering and casting long distances for big wily chub that are jittery and easily frightened, it is best to remain well back from the bank, low down and out of sight. The lightest possible leger weight should be used so that a cast can be made to the approximate area where the chub are thought to lie. The tackle should then be allowed, or assisted by rod tip raising, to roll or bounce with the current into the final desired position.

In sharp contrast to the 'seek them out and catch them' tactics I have just described, it is also possible to catch chub by remaining completely immobile. If an angler is willing to sit and exercise a great deal of patience, he can often establish himself in a quiet slack and by judicious groundbaiting into the main current, draw a whole shoal of chub into his chosen area and steadily catch them all day long.

Grayling

All rivers are not blessed, or cursed as some trout fishing purists would describe it, by that beautiful fish 'drop-out', the grayling. This has been welcomed into the ranks of the coarse fish species because of its spawning period, which coincides with other species. In addition to the pleasurable sport it gives on the end of a line, it is the one fish of all the twelve listed here (eels excepted, for they are delicious) which I have eaten with relish and then yearned for more. I have painfully waded my way through almost all the rest and have only two words to describe them— gastronomically atrocious!

Grayling like clean, pellucid streams and rivers, especially those high-quality chalk stream trout waters with an abundant growth of streamer weed and a gravel bottom. Their appearance is quite unmistakable as no other fish with a comparable dorsal fin exists in our fresh waters. The top growth weight range of the grayling is hard to define. For a very long time $4\frac{1}{2}$ lbs. was considered about the maximum, then a fish of just over 7 lbs. was reported caught in a Scottish river. Strange to relate, no grayling anywhere near that weight has been caught since, and twenty years have now elapsed. A three pounder is a very big grayling indeed and the angler who manages to catch fish in the 1–2 lb. weight bracket can feel highly satisfied with his performance and also the water where such fish are present.

'Trotting the stream' with the small gilt-tail worm is the recognized traditional method of fishing for grayling. During the colder months of the year, from about late September right through the winter until the coarse fishing season closes, good sport with this fish can be had in the most freezing weather conditions, when little else on the river is moving or showing the slightest inclination to feed. However, there is always a possibility that a shoal of good roach may be encountered whilst you are fishing for grayling and that several may be found in your landing net before the grayling start to come again. Conversely, it is not unusual to find the odd grayling here and there when fishing for roach. They often move quite some distance upstream in pursuit of the odd 'loose feed' maggots that have been wafted along by the current.

Roach style trotting tackle can safely be employed for the usual run of grayling in the 1–2 lb. class but special mention must be made of the suitability of the 'traditional' grayling 'bob' float. It is a round cork abomination with a short wooden peg stuck through a hole in the middle of the small, pike style 'bung'; as a practical bite indicator its efficiency is nil. It will bob, as its name implies, and jitter but it offers so much resistance to a delicate bite that it is best left in the tackle box— or better still the tackle shop—as an archaic, useless, museum piece.

The most efficient floats for this fishing are those with buoyancy aloft and plenty of stability down below. The modern, wire stemmed, balsa bodied, grayling trotting floats fill the bill admirably, both for fishing in ruffled and in calm waters. When properly made they are entirely self-cocking, so that if desired, a slow sinking bait effect can be achieved without the use of even a dust shot.

Really big grayling, those dim, flitting shapes which you see hovering momentarily over light chalk patches and estimate to be well over 3 or 4 lbs., are most difficult fish to catch. Trotting a worm down to them on float tackle seldom rouses their interest. If they are in a group of three or four they delicately move aside and let the worm pass quite close to them without showing the slightest inclination to sample it.

'Free lined' offerings of bread, worm or maggots are often taken by big grayling when the angler is working down a fast water stretch for chub or barbel. However, large grayling have also been taken on small livebaits and trout spinners, so that the field is wide open to experiment by any angler who fancies his chances.

Before we leave the grayling, a word or two on the subject of their preparation and cooking. At the risk of offending all domestic refrigerator manufacturers and those who advocate their widespread use for keeping fish fresh, I will fearlessly declare that a fine fresh fish flavour and ice are completely incompatible. The first is destroyed by the second, therefore they should not be brought together.

Prepare your grayling fresh from the water. Cook and eat it the same day to get the full benefit of its culinary delicacy. Fish that are about 10 to 12 ozs. are best. They should be gutted and have their heads, fins and tails removed; then they should be washed in cold water and dried, rolled in flour, and fried in hot, deep fat until their skins are brown and crackly. Served with lemon juice or melted butter and eaten by a pleasantly tired angler whose appetite has been sharpened by a crisp, clear November day on the river, they are food for the gods.

Barbel

Since the beginning of the 1950s, the coarse fishing scene has been completely dominated by two fish: barbel and carp. Certain anglers have been fired with such an abiding enthusiasm for them, that they have forsaken the pursuit of any other species in order to concentrate their efforts solely upon one or the other of these fish. In this section I shall deal with the barbel, and appropriately, a discourse on carp will follow in the next.

Barbel are very special, lively, strong, hard fighting fish and the soundest of equipment is needed to catch them in their fast-flowing, deep-water habitat. It must always be borne in mind that these fish *cannot* be taken on tackle which would quite adequately cope with still-water species of a similar size. Pound for pound, a barbel in the peak of condition will outstrip anything 'on fins' in our British fresh waters.

A good 'Avon' rod and fixed-spool or centre-pin reel, carrying a 5 or 6 lb. line will fill the bill for the general run of barbel up to a weight of 10 lbs. But what about those 'chance of a lifetime' heavyweight fish? The monsters which are thought to run right up to the 20 lb. mark. Barbel specialists have designed their own rods for these leviathans. The rods are almost always in hollow glass, in two pieces, and about 11 ft. long. They are intended for use with lines near the 10 lb. mark. One essential feature which they all incorporate is a very long, slim cork handle, the butt of which can be tucked under the armpit, whilst the rest of it lays along the forearm. In this way the wrist does not take the brunt of a prolonged tussle with a big fish.

The rolling leger is a well-tried method of angling for barbel. It is a very simple rig. Merely thread an Arlesey bomb of a suitable weight (according to your estimation of the power of flow of the river) up the reel line and stop it a couple of feet from the end by a swan shot; then finish off the terminal tackle assembly with a suitable eyed or spade-end hook of a size which will mount the intended bait correctly.

When you cast your tackle upstream you are 'upstream legering' but once the tackle bumps and rolls its way past the imaginary line drawn from where you are sitting to the opposite bank, you are deemed to be 'downstream legering'. There are many subtle differences which must be taken into consideration when you fish either the upstream or downstream leger and these must always be studied seriously if either method is to prove effective. One golden rule for any sort of legering is that you should use the least possible amount of lead on all occasions.

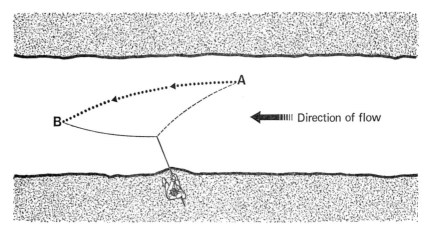

38. *Rolling Leger Method.*
Tackle is cast upstream to A and allowed to bump and roll downstream to B.

The pressure of the water and the line will move a rolling leger from one resting place to the next. As it must always move around in a natural manner, a little experimenting with different weights of bomb should be carried out so that a perfect balance is obtained. If there is too much weight, the leger will be static and only be moved by a fish taking the bait, or the angler raising his rod tip and lifting the bomb off the bottom. If there is too little weight, it will not come to rest at all, but trundle along quite fast, through the swim in a 'free-lined' fashion, which may not be the effect the angler intended.

When leger tackle is cast upstream, the press of the current on the line puts a bow in it, and this can be watched as a means of bite indication. Also, when a fish takes the bait, it sometimes shifts the leger weight and drops back with the current towards the angler. This is known as a 'slack-line' bite.

When you cast your leger tackle downstream the line is pulled tight by the flow. Bites are now signalled by rapid bangs on the taut line and rod end. Some will be so strong that the rod will jerk in your hand or be rattled sharply if it is in a rest.

Recently, 'maggot saturation' groundbaiting methods have been practised on some barbel rivers and good sport has resulted. Unfortunately, the barbel are now so preoccupied with maggots that they have become 'one food fish', spurning the old, long-established baits of bread, worms, cheese and sausage. This maggot mania has brought about a curious bait situation for intending barbel anglers. A piscatorial 'closed shop' policy exists: use maggots or no fish!

'Long trotting' is a most pleasant high-summer method of taking the average-sized barbel. If a shallowish 'wading' swim can be found where the angler (suitably clad in thigh boots) can position himself among the streamer weeds with his back to the current and trot his tackle downstream, the finest of all action sport can be had.

Capacious landing nets for barbel are essential but any ideas of keeping several barbel in a keep-net should be abandoned. After their prolonged and weakening fight, barbel are usually in no fit state to be returned immediately or bundled into a keep net in the hope that they will recover. They invariably need a little assistance from a considerate angler. Gently hold them in the current, fully submerged, until they regain their strength and are able to swim quite strongly away.

Carp

In all the other sections on coarse fish, I have usually described suitable tackle for catching them but as far as carp are concerned, especially the giants of 20 lbs. or more, it would be much more appropriate if I suggested tackle for *attempting* to catch them with!

At the outset, it would be as well if the angling beginner realized just how difficult it is to catch carp. Dedicated, experienced carp fishers count their captures not in fish per session, but sometimes in fish per season. On difficult waters in which perhaps only a dozen or so very big carp live, the yardstick of success may well be measured in bites or runs per season, with just the odd carp actually taken after months of intensive fishing.

There are two species of carp. The Common carp, which has been caught at a figure of 44 lbs. but is estimated to attain at least the 50 lb.

mark, and a lesser breed, known as the Crucian carp which attains a top weight of about 3 or 4 lbs. Common carp have several sub-divisions. There are wild carp, a lightweight, slimly built variety which go up to about 10 lbs., and also King carp which are usually of Continental origin or strain, and imported for their phenomenal growth rate. King carp further subdivide into Leather and Mirror carp. In carp angler's jargon it is possible to take 'wildies', 'commons', 'leathers' and 'mirrors', with perhaps the odd diminutive 'crucian' thrown in for good measure.

As a very rough and ready guide, crucian carp are chubby and rather bream-like and have no barbules. Wild carp are fully scaled and streamlined. Common carp are also fully scaled but of heavier proportions and grow very large. Leathers appear scaleless or perhaps have just a few scales near the tail. Mirror carp have a few large scales, usually along and above the lateral line, that resemble mirrors. All these varieties of Common carp have four barbules, two quite large ones located at each corner of the mouth and a pair of smaller ones just above the top lip.

The Crucian carp can be instantly dismissed for it can be taken on ordinary light roach tackle, but the rest of the carp family require something very special in the way of rods, reels, lines, hooks and even landing nets. The angler too, needs a psychological approach to carp fishing. This is often described by non-anglers as fanaticism, especially when they have viewed winter carp enthusiasts nonchalantly sitting it out in the frost and snow of a mid-winter night.

Carp rods are invariably 10 ft. long, in two pieces, and made of only the best split cane or hollow glass. The fixed-spool reel is, without a doubt, the one for carp fishing. It should be fully loaded, almost to the spool lip, with line in the 8 to 12 lb. breaking strain range. As for barbel fishing, mount the reel well up the long cork handle so that a 'tuck' under the rod armpit can be made with the butt for added control and extra leverage. This helps when the forearm is getting tired and trembly during a prolonged battle with a weighty fish.

Hooks are of paramount importance. You will find special carp hooks on sale in the tackle shops. They are eyed, very well made and rather expensive. Two or three in each size from 10 to 2 will suffice for an initial stock.

Good carp waters which hold monster specimens are few and far between, but due to the sudden popularity of carp fishing in the early

39. *Carp Tackle. Silver paper indicator on line before and after (arrowed) a 'run' when the fish takes the bait.*

A

1950s many waters have since been stocked with carp and have the makings of excellent carp fisheries. Whilst I am aware that every angler dreams of huge carp wallowing in lily-padded lagoons of which he has the sole fishing rights, it is more realistic to assume that you will probably find yourself seated by a rather featureless gravel pit which is completely weedless and not unlike one of the craters on the moon!

Two baits reign supreme in the carp angler's world; bread and soft boiled potatoes. Worms are another very good carp bait, especially when 'free lined' off the bottom as 'floaters'. However, down below they have the obnoxious habit of attracting large, tangle producing eels, and believe me, the height of panic to a placid carp angler, is a great big eel hooked after dark!

Practically all carp angling is done with 'free lined', weightless tackle. In order to hook the carp which usually picks up the bait and makes off with it at speed (this is known as a run), it is best to set up the rod on two rests, after the bait has been cast out, and the 'pick-up' on the fixed-spool reel moved into the 'off' position. The line can then run out freely. During daylight hours this exciting movement takes place before your very eyes, and plays havoc with your nerves. After dark, some form of bite indicator is necessary. The simplest method is a square of silver paper folded over the line, just below the first rod ring; the most sophisticated is a buzzing, flashing-light electric bite alarm.

One last grim warning about such gadgets. A friend of mine, using one for the first time in conjunction with a very comfortable bed chair, dozed off . . . When the buzzer sounded, he thought he was at home in bed and that his alarm clock was going off. Leaping out of his make-shift bed to switch it off, he landed up to his waist in four feet of muddy, ice-cold water!

Pike

It is very unwise to deliberately fish for pike if you are frightened to handle them or bear them any great malice. Either way, your judgement will be clouded by fear or hate when you have them at your mercy in a landing net, or impaled on a gaff. Therefore, unless you view the pike in a dispassionate manner, as a large and naturally ferocious fish, it is best to leave them strictly alone and leave your image as a sporting angler intact.

There are three popular methods of taking pike: with livebait, dead-bait or artificials, i.e. spinners or lures. The first has come in for a great deal of criticism and is banned on some waters. The second is quite innocuous and at times unbelievably effective, and the last is now begin-ning to catch on everywhere and attract more devotees than the other two put together.

Except for certain differences in the terminal rigs and the fact that floats are seldom used for deadbaiting the tackle used for livebaiting and deadbaiting can be identical. A fairly long, flexible and powerful rod is necessary to cast a dead or live fish in the region of 8 ozs. to a couple of pounds. Such rods are usually two piece, about 10 ft. in length and specially built for the job. Reels can be centre-pin, fixed-spool or even a light sea multiplier, but they must all be capable of handling a line in the 10 to 15 lb. range and of sufficient spool capacity to take at least 200 yards of it.

Originally, floats for livebaiting were of the 'Angling Cartoon' type, i.e. round, large and gaily painted. Today, they are streamlined, unobtrusive and offer little resistance to a taking fish. They are matched to bait sizes. It is essential that the float shall only just support the fish bait so that the livebait can work naturally without tiring itself out by dragging an outsize buoy around in its wake.

Terminal rigs for pike should always incorporate swivels and wire, either the single strand sort or the softer, more pliable kind. After many and varied experiments with multi-hook terminal rigs for both live and

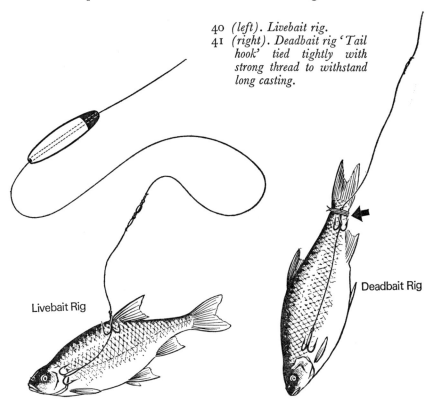

40 *(left). Livebait rig.*
41 *(right). Deadbait rig 'Tail hook' tied tightly with strong thread to withstand long casting.*

Livebait Rig

Deadbait Rig

deadbaiting, I have found that the two-hook Jardine snap tackle gives a good all round performance so far as bait retaining and pike hooking and holding are concerned. You will probably also dabble with large single hooks, trebles and endless combinations and permutations of the two, as you endeavour to mount your live or deadbait in a presentable manner and try to ensure that the pike is securely hooked in the mouth the moment it picks up the bait.

Livebaiting is a very deadly method for densely weeded water when spinning would be impossible and deadbaiting impracticable, due to a dense growth of bottom weed. The float can be adjusted so that the bait is set to swim just above the weeds. This tackle has the added advantage of being able to be dropped into the smallest of 'dustbin' lid sized holes with impunity. The snags to this kind of fishing are sometimes infuriating, the most serious being the inability to obtain bait of the right sort at the right time. Unless the livebaiter has a garden pool or large tank which he keeps well filled with a standby stock of roach, dace, rudd, small perch and bream, he will often find himself frantically fishing with light tackle for such livebait, whilst all around him the pike are going mad and taking anything that moves.

Deadbaiting with 'free-line' tackle, i.e. bait at the end of the line, fished on a reasonably clear bottom, is a 'rod-in-rest' relaxing brand of angling. At times it is the only method which will take pike that are lying low in the water and sulking, perhaps with poor appetites. Deadbaits can be 'trotted' on rivers if they are suspended from a float. By far the best method is to allow them to drift downstream right to the edge, alongside the reeds. Should they come to rest do not immediately disturb them by reeling in, let them linger for a little while. Many a good lurking pike has been taken in just such a situation.

By far the most active, dare I suggest attractive method of taking pike is the modern 'Sportfishing' or 'Spinfishing' style which has attained tremendous popularity lately. Rods for this type of angling can be the orthodox 7–10 ft. spinning rods of British origin or the American designed, ultra-short 'crank-handled' bait casters around the 5 ft. mark. When used in conjunction with a suitably sized multiplier reel and line, these can lift much of the old 'cast and retrieve' drudgery. In recent years they have brought many big fish on to the bank and made the 'spin low and spin slow' diehards sit up, take note and ponder.

A final word about whether you should land your pike with a gaff or a landing net. Landing nets, if very large are quite humane, but some awful problems can arise when they are being used. The main trouble occurs when a loose hook outside the mouth of the pike gets caught in the meshes of the net before the fish is inside it. You then have the panic of a threshing pike tearing its jaws to shreds whilst firmly attached to an outsize net. Gaffs seem barbarous instruments but if the pike is neatly gaffed through the bottom jaw from inside to the outside, it will suffer no harm. Avoid gaffing from underneath the bottom jaw as this drives the hook up into the top jaw as well.

The unhooking of small pike will generally give no problems. Those up to about 10 lbs. can usually be enveloped in a piece of rough, wet sacking and worked on with ease. However, it is when you start to take pike of the heavyweight class, in the region of 20, 30 or, if you have phenomenal luck, 40 lbs., that your troubles will really begin. If you do hook a big pike deeply, way back in the gullet and the hooks are out of sight, on no account attempt extensive bankside surgery to recover them. Snip the wire trace as near to the offending hooks as possible and release the fish immediately. This may sound rather callous but it is by far the best action you can take. Left to its own devices, the pike will rid itself of the hooks much quicker than you would imagine and most probably recover. In your hands, out of water, and facing a lengthy hook removal operation it is doomed from the outset.

Eels

I have purposely left eels until last because I consider them to be such an enigmatic quarry that they require a completely separate line of mental approach and tackle. What other freshwater fish of 5 lb. weight can so impress an angler with its strength that he quite soberly tackles up for it with the best of pike or heavy duty carp rods and a line in the 10, 15 or even 20 lb. range?

Eels are everywhere. They find their way into the most inaccessible places, and the really big ones, those in excess of 5 lbs. and up to 10, 12, or as much as 15 lbs., are the devil's own job to locate or observe. It has been established beyond doubt that the monsters of the eel kingdom are barren females, or perhaps frustrated females that cannot return to the sea to follow their natural pattern of life because they are unable to leave the water in which they live.

How then do we go about finding a big eel water? Firstly, I think it is safe to say, by ruling out all the little eel waters! There are then three distinct methods to consider and they should all be given a fair trial when the locating of big eels is being attempted. The easiest of the three is to sound the angling 'grape-vine' until you hear of a water where outsize eels are regularly caught. Alternatively, you can concentrate on a water where quite a number of medium-sized eels have been caught and hope that you will be successful in taking much bigger ones. Finally, and this is the best method of the three, you can choose a water which is reputed to hold lots of small fish—roach, perch, etc., but nothing else. If the forecast is proved correct, you will have drawn a dismal blank and will have to start all over again, but if the water contains a very few, extra large, hitherto unknown eels all your trouble will have been worthwhile.

Generally speaking, still waters—ponds, lakes and canals—seem to be better big eel producers than rivers. Prolific eel waters will rarely be found to have the real whoppers in them. A superabundance of small eels does not make for excessive growth as there is too much vying for food. If you fish such a water you will be assured of the ingredients for many eel pies, but a rapid succession of half pounders will drive the big eel seeker to distraction.

The eel-catching season is rather a short one and occurs during the summer months, but this is probably a good thing in view of the fact that outsize eels are very nocturnal in their activities and the angler has to be at the waterside during the hours of darkness to take them. From about 10 p.m. to the early hours of the morning, just before dawn, has proved to be the eel's peak feeding time.

Before we go into the finer points of tackle, baits and methods, there are certain items of equipment which must first be considered for big eel fishing. These are all very necessary once the eel has been well and truly hooked and is being brought to the bank. Nothing can throw an otherwise level-headed angler into a blind panic than a good, big lively eel, caught in the dark. Therefore, some sort of low-level, all-round illumination is necessary when the tussle starts. A hand held torch is useless. Even if there are two of you, all four hands may be needed. A shaded electric inspection lamp on a metal stand which can be stuck into the bank is ideal.

A really mammoth, deep, fine meshed landing net is necessary to engulf large eels, but where the bank is gently sloping they can be slid up it if reasonably played out. I will refrain from the folly of even hinting that an eel can ever be described as 'spent' because it never is. The safest procedure, once the eel is banked, is to get it quickly into a large open weave sack, tie the mouth tight and cut the line. You can leave it either in the water tethered to a stout stick if you wish to return it alive, or on the bank, still tethered, so that both eel and sack are not inclined to 'wander off', if you intend eating the eel; then carry on fishing, leaving the tricky task of unhooking, weighing and measuring until daylight.

Tackle for eels must be very strong but never coarse or cumbersome, as the eel is a delicate feeder and will not tolerate resistance in the shape of heavy lead weights or stiff, hawser-like wire traces. A light 10 or 11 ft. short handled beach caster in hollow glass will tame most eels, especially if used in conjunction with a sea multiplier or a large fixed-spool reel. Sound pike livebaiting or deadbaiting tackle is also ideal. At the risk of

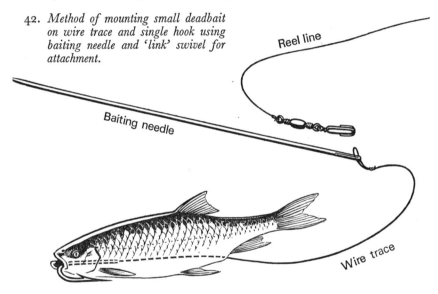

42. *Method of mounting small deadbait on wire trace and single hook using baiting needle and 'link' swivel for attachment.*

Reel line

Baiting needle

Wire trace

being ridiculed, I would suggest nothing less than a 15 lb. line and perhaps up to 20 or even 30 lb. if the water is really overgrown or snaggy and the eels monstrous!

Wire terminal tackles are essential for eels. They should be of a slightly lower breaking strain than the line and mounted with two swivels—a plain one for attachment to the reel line and a split link swivel for easy hook attachment when deadbaits are threaded on with a baiting needle. The all important hook should be suited in size to the bait. Sizes 2, 4 or 6 for bunches of lobworms and even larger sea hooks for deadbaits.

It is fatal to use cheap, poorly tempered hooks for eels as they get an awful amount of twisting due to the eel's characteristic writhing motion when it is being played, not to mention its violent antics when it has been hauled out of the water.

Opinions are sharply divided when expert, big eel exponents begin to argue the merits of the two most popular baits: dead fish and large worms. Some say that a quicker strike is possible with worms because the eel is able to mouth such a bait more easily, others argue that a 3 or 4 in. deadbait will sort out the big eels from the lesser ones because it is a fair sized offering which will appeal to them.

Whatever your choice of bait, make sure that the rod is in two rests after casting out and that the pick-up is in the 'off' position so that the line can flow out freely when a 'run' occurs. With a worm bait, some anglers tighten up the line after casting, disengage the pick-up on the reel and then strike immediately the line begins to peel off the reel spool. They sweep up the rod, engage the pick-up with a swift flick of the reel handle and swing the rod tip up, and well back over their shoulder. However, when using dead fish baits, where the wire trace has been threaded through the fish from the vent, with the hook situated near the head, it is customary to let the eel have its first run and then strike when it pauses, on the assumption that it is in the act of turning the bait in its jaws and is about to swallow it head first.

Trial and error is the only way to gain experience in these difficult fields of specialized angling, especially when it carries the added hazard of being done in the dark! In all free-line fishing for the larger coarse fish species, one important point should be borne in mind. Rods should never, under any circumstances be left unattended to 'fish themselves', and most certainly not with the reel pick-up engaged. Failure to observe this simple rule may one day result in the amazing spectacle of a full set of valuable tackle suddenly shooting lakewards as a large fish takes the bait and powerfully heaves the lot into the water against the solid resistance of an 'in gear' reel.

Other Small Coarse Fish

Apart from the dozen main species of coarse fish dealt with in this chapter, there are lesser kinds which are not very important as they do not attain a weight in excess of a few ounces. Some of them, the gudgeon, minnow and bleak, are suitable as livebaits, but to the serious angler they are not worthy of much consideration. At times, however, during fishing matches, when weightier coarse fish such as bream and roach are hard to come by, a mixed bag of bleak, gudgeon, ruffe, bullheads and even minnows, will enable the harassed competitors to put some sort of a weight on to the scales and thereby save the whole business from becoming a fishless farce.

Fishing the Whole Year Through

It is quite natural, when you first approach coarse fishing, to think of it only as a fine weather, lazy, summer pastime which begins about the middle of June and ends when the Autumn leaves start to fall, but should you limit your angling to this period and pack away your tackle when the first nip starts to be felt in the morning air, you will miss some of the best fish catching times of the whole year. The mild, late autumn, mid-winter and very early spring periods, can often be far more productive than the short mid-summer holiday season when the waters are apt to be crowded.

The angler who rates his own personal comfort of paramount importance, and to that end partakes of his fishing only during office hours (9 a.m. to 5 p.m.) will certainly spend some most recuperative times by the waterside, dozing peacefully in the bright sunlight when the weather is hot. However, he is hardly likely to take great catches in such brassy conditions because to be a successful angler it is necessary, at all times, to give first consideration to the fish and their many moods.

Good fishing and a bright sun, high in the sky, do not seem to mix. At odd times, this piscine prophecy does not hold good and some astounding catches are made, but taken over a fair period, early morning and late evening fishing during the summer months will definitely be found to produce better catches than the 'sun up', middle of the day period. Once we start to consider what is really meant by the terms early morning and late evening, we begin to overlap the times, run one into the other, and end up fishing all night. On warm summer nights, when the hours of darkness are only very few, this can be wonderful.

Let me qualify this term 'night fishing', as there are three distinct kinds which can be practised according to the amount of inconvenience and lack of sleep which the angler is prepared to suffer. First there is

what I will call 'Late Night Fishing'. This is merely an after dark extension of a late afternoon and evening spell, when the fish go on feeding
and you stay with them until they stop biting—perhaps about midnight
or a little after. Second is 'Genuine All Night Fishing'. The angler gets
established by the waterside well before darkness comes, fishes con-
tinuously till daylight and then packs up for home and bed an hour or
so after dawn. Last, but most popular, is the bed-chair or car snoozing
style of angling which I will call 'Interrupted Night Fishing'. You move
into position at the waterside with your gear during the late afternoon
or early evening and fish whilst the quarry are feeding. If there is a lull
in the activity, or you feel drowsy, you have a sleep for two or three
hours on your waterside bed or in the car if it can be parked handily,
then resume fishing just before dawn when a further fish movement or
'feeding cycle' will most probably start.

There are three main rules to observe for comfortable, pleasurable
night fishing. One is to know your waters and be able to choose a venue
which is sheltered and has a suitable bank for setting up your equipment.
The second is that this equipment is more than adequate to keep you
and your tackle dry should a prolonged downpour occur. The third,
and most important is that the angler should be stocked up with food,
creature comforts and spare clothing so that hunger and thirst can be
immediately assuaged and the slightest inclination to shiver removed by
a rapid putting on of extra garments.

Good night-fishing companions are very rare. They either make
themselves so comfortable and cosy that they instantly fall sound asleep
and snore loudly, or are so nervous of the dark and the scuffling and
the unidentifiable waterside noises that they abandon their tackle and
crouch by your side the whole time, chatting feverishly, whistling or
humming, apparently to stave off the terrors of the night!

The subject of illumination whilst you are fishing in the dark is a very
knotty problem. Some experienced 'night owls' can operate their tackle
on all but the most pitch black night. Other anglers who are not so
adept at keeping their gear free from snags and tangles feel more con-
fident with just a bare glimmer of light the whole time. Electric torches
and lamps are very fine when the batteries are fresh but they are apt to
leave you in the lurch just when you need them most. Also, it is vital
that a spare set of batteries and a bulb are always to hand.

The most economical light source I have been able to find, after a long search, is an ordinary, cheap hardware store hurricane lamp. One filling of paraffin will last about 12 hours and the running cost is negligible. What makes them ideal is the fact that the brightness of the light source can be adjusted over a very wide range. You can have quite a bright light or a really dim one by the simple expedient of turning the wick up or down. To shield such lights from the water, if you have a theory that light should not shine upon it whilst you fish, fit them around one side with a tin shield, wired on to keep it in place.

In some parts of the country night fishing is strictly prohibited and frowned upon, but on quite a number of waters it is allowed and recognized as a very necessary part of the angling scene. In order that such a privilege remains with us there is a common-sense code of behaviour which should be observed at all times. Always arrive and set up for all night angling during broad daylight if possible, with the minimum amount of fuss so far as car door banging and boot lid slamming is concerned. Arrange to stay put the whole time and move out again silently in daylight. If, for any reason, your start is delayed or you finish a session in the dark and have to move off the water at an hour when all non-angling folk are safely tucked away in bed, for goodness sake be quiet and give them every consideration. If you go lumbering through a farmyard in a roistering band with torches flashing, some of you could lose the seat of your pants to a watchful dog, or worse still, be threatened by a farmer's loaded shotgun especially if it is late in the year, around turkey fattening time!

Apart from the brief three months of the close season—mid-March to mid-June—when actual fishing is curtailed, the ardent coarse fisherman can begin his angling on Open Season day in high summer and fish his way right through the best part of four seasons: Summer, Autumn, Winter and early Spring. Each month has its own special appeal and to patiently observe the passing of a whole year in the countryside whilst fishing out-of-doors in all weathers gives one a rare appreciation of the wonders of nature which are all too often missed in the hurly burly of a busy life, most of which is spent within the confines of four walls.

Anglers have their own very special personal calendar on which the names of the months are not nearly so important as the fish which they pursue about that time. June the 16th, Open Season Day, usually means tench, but weeks before that time, a great weed clearing, swim preparing and baiting up campaign may have taken place. If the nights have been warm and damp, many anglers with torches and cycle lamps will have crawled around lawns, bowling greens and golf courses in pursuit of that universal fish catcher, the lobworm. In the excitement of the chase, trousers knees will have become muddy and damp and a great creaking and cracking of the joints will be heard when these anglers carefully lower themselves on to their baskets by the misty tench pools on that first magical morn.

The carp addicts will also have been very busy preparing the ground for another summer of long, silent vigils by reedy pools. For them the first few warm days of the close season will mean fish watching. Sometimes from lofty perches in tall trees with binoculars, or hidden deep among the bankside foliage with polaroid spectacles to note every underwater detail and movement which is revealed.

During the summer, there are so many fish to pursue that a very disciplined mind has to be brought into action to prevent a rapid, unproductive flitting from water to water style of angling being practiced. Contrary to the false, but long retained belief that pike are not worth fishing for until there have been some good frosts and ice has formed in the night on the margins, these fish are in fine fettle right from the start of the season. It is actually in the closing weeks—late February and early March—when some heavyweight females are liable to be hooked when they are sluggish and full of spawn that the angler should show a sensible regard for their condition and refrain from taking them.

Each new season brings a first great rush of enthusiasm which is hard to control. After weeks of water watching and tackle renovating, the angler is at last free to start fishing in deadly earnest and often there seems hardly time to sleep. Perhaps still-water tench or carp are concentrated upon for the first few days, but then at weekends, if the weather is fine, some evening roach, rudd or barbel river sessions will be arranged —to the detriment of your sleep quota, especially if you have been up very early the same day fishing on a gravel pit or lake.

Once the ball has started to roll and you come into contact with other keen fishermen, all exchanging ideas and telling of good catches, this mid-summer madness is liable to grip you like a fever so that you wish, more than anything to fish continually, to the exclusion of all else in life.

Happily, with the coming of Autumn, the scene changes a little and the pressure to pursue many species of coarse fish is alleviated, due to the fact that some of them fade into the depths or become dormant. In still waters, unless we have a long, exceptionally mild Indian Summer— about the end of September, carp, tench and eels can be written off until the warmer weather arrives again; on the rivers, barbel mysteriously make themselves scarce with the advent of the first frosts. However, as a special bonus, the grayling comes to the fore about this time and with the dying of the weeds, river pike begin to be very active.

Winter is the true 'long trotting' season when roach, dace and chub can be taken even in the most unpleasant weather. Sometimes on still waters, in the very depths of winter, a few days of warm winds and a 'muggy' atmosphere will bring the fish to life so that all sorts of unusual catches are made. Tench and carp appear near the surface and begin to roll about; the pike go mad; and roach, perch and rudd become more active and feed for just a day or so as they did in the height of the summer.

One great boon of mid-winter fishing which offsets the cold, wet and discomfort, is the 'late rising' factor. To be at the water at the crack of dawn in summer means such an early start that it is hardly worth going to bed. The long winter nights, however, are more kind to the lie-abed angler who can rise at the very late hour of seven o'clock and still be on the water for first light around 8 a.m. Likewise, an eight-hour mid-winter angling session can begin just on first light and finish for a five o'clock tea without any early rising or late homecoming being involved.

To enjoy winter fishing, it is absolutely essential to remain warm and dry the whole time. Masses of woollies are useless if they are not worn under really waterproof, light, unrestricting outerwear. Rubber boots, either knee or thigh length, should be purchased at least one size too big to allow for ample sock room. Some all weather angling types prefer a knee-length jacket and thigh waders. Others swear by knee boots, with waterproof trousers and a rather shorter coat. In really wet, foul, cold weather, hats and scarves are useless. The only article of clothing which will protect that important neck and ear area is an anorak style garment with a waterproof, fur-lined hood. It must have a drawstring so that the whole affair can be snugged down tight round the face and neck and underneath the chin, sealing off the nape of the neck and preventing cold drips from running down inside the collar.

On winter rivers, when the water is higher than normal and well coloured, quite a large bait can be used in the slower flowing sections and the backflows or slacks. Worms are always worth a trial under these conditions and bread flake—a piece the size of your thumb-nail on a 10 or 12 hook—can be deadly for roach and chub if fished stationary, right on the bottom in the very quiet, slack water where there are deep holes right under the bank.

A very low, clear river in winter calls for finer tackle and smaller baits than one which is running high, fast and coloured. Also the concealment aspect has to be taken into consideration a great deal more when every frond of weed and stone is clearly visible.

By using the three valuable close season months as a time for exploration, depth testing and water mapping, the resourceful angler need never be worried by adverse winter weather conditions. Should he arrive to fish a river and find it raging along and over its banks, the colour of thick, brown cocoa, he can always switch to the nearest still-water venue and get himself settled into a swim without having to carry out the extensive survey which is often necessary when an unknown water is visited for the first time.

CHAPTER 6

MORE ADVANCED TACKLE
AND EQUIPMENT

O NE wonderful thing about the whole world of angling, and coarse fishing in particular, is the absolutely unhampered, free flow of information and ideas which are continually passing to and fro between its devotees. No true angler of an active, enquiring mind can ever overcome the intense curiosity he feels whenever he sees someone fishing. And if the person observed is using an item of tackle which is original, new fangled or even outlandish in design, there is no peace of mind until it has been thoroughly examined, discussed and its performance demonstrated.

These waterside chats, which sometimes develop into rather lengthy discourses, are the very essence of angling education. The coarse fishing beginner who is still in the initial stages of trying to master the very strange tackle he has assembled, will have a strong desire to hide himself away in lonely places until he becomes familiar with it. However, a quiet walk around the water before and after fishing will often be very beneficial, as it will acquaint the novice with all the latest tackle and methods which are being used.

When to leger and when to use the float is a stumbling block which constantly bothers most anglers, whether they are very experienced or just raw recruits. Water depth, speed of flow and weather conditions usually govern this tedious problem and if observed closely they will help you to decide instantly. If you require your bait to be presented slap-bang on the bottom of a fast-flowing river, it is no use trying to get it there and keep it in place by means of float tackle—a leger is the thing to use. Again, should you wish to fish for big perch or roach with large lobworms in a forty foot deep gravel pit, and expect to take them on the bottom, then a leger is once more necessary.

Floats are very sensitive means of visual bite indication but they will only be effective under certain conditions. A very wind-blown, turbulent water surface makes the watching of a float most difficult. If there is sunlight on the water one can experience eye-strain, even when polaroid glasses are worn. To fish at a great distance—60 or 70 yards—may require a heavy float which will flight smoothly through the air and present a large, above-surface area that can easily be seen. In such circumstances a light leger on a fine line may do a better job.

The 'Lift' method

Occasionally, a special method has been evolved to provide the answer to a particular angling problem and no other style of angling will work as effectively. As you become more experienced you will add to your repertoire and eventually feel completely at home in all kinds of trying circumstances.

Apart from the two well-known float methods—bait lying on the bottom or suspended somewhere higher up in the water—three other float techniques should be tried when the conditions demand them. For very shy-biting fish which are feeding in a fickle manner over a clean, firm bottom, a still-water technique known as the 'lift' method may prove an answer to the problem. In order that the tackle may be set up correctly, a plummet should be used to ascertain the exact depth. The float is secured by the bottom only and cocked by just one shot placed about half an inch from the hook. After the tackle has been cast out to the precise spot where the depth test was made, it is allowed to settle. The rod is then placed in two rests and the line tightened till just the barest tip of the float is visible above the water surface. From that moment on, any disturbance of the bait will release the weight on the float and it will rise up in the water, usually to the amazement of the angler who is using this very sensitive bite indication method for the first time. The secret to setting up the tackle for this float style is to obtain a balance between the single shot which is just resting on the bottom, and the float. The weight of this one shot should be just enough to cock the float but never so heavy as to give the slightest amount of resistance to a taking fish.

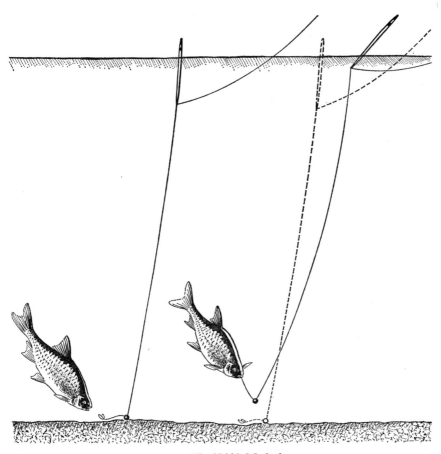

43. *The 'Lift' Method.*

Slider Floats

If it is necessary to fish with a float in water that is much too deep to enable the tackle to be cast easily, due to the fact that a greater length of line is suspended beneath the float than the measurement of the rod, a slider float should be used. This is an ordinary pattern of float, fairly large and buoyant, with a tall stem 4 or 5 in. long projecting upwards from a squat body. The single bottom attaching ring for the line is very fine, well formed and just allows the line to pass freely through

99

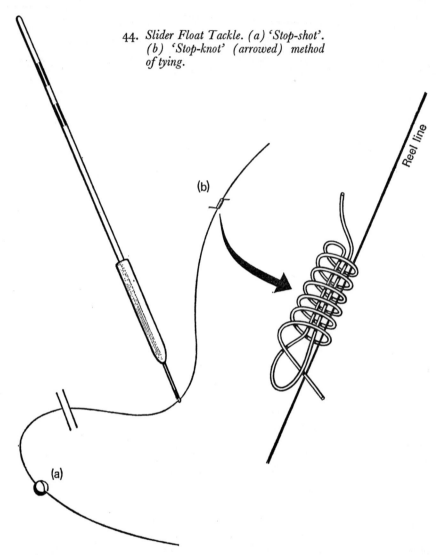

44. *Slider Float Tackle. (a) 'Stop-shot'. (b) 'Stop-knot' (arrowed) method of tying.*

(b)

Reel line

(a)

it. A nylon 'stop knot' which is just too large to pass through the eye of the float, but small enough to go through the rod rings easily, is tied to the reel line at the appropriate depth at which the bait is required to be suspended. When the tackle is being cast, the slider float slips down the line and stops at the uppermost split shot, which can be 3 or 4 ft. above the hook. As the terminal tackle enters the water, the weight of the bait and shot pull the line through the bottom ring of the float until it is checked at the required depth by the stop knot. Slider floats are very useful for fishing deep water when it is necessary for the bait to be suspended just above thick bottom weeds or a deep carpet of mud.

Float legering

Float legering is a combination of the two techniques. It seems to have fallen out of favour these days but for slow flowing water, especially when bream are the quarry, it is ideal. The terminal tackle is very simple—a tied direct hook, a small bored bullet slotted on to the line and stopped at an appropriate distance from the hook with a single split-shot, and the float of your choice mounted above it, usually attached by the bottom ring only. This rig allows the bait to be fished right on the bottom in a stationary position. The idea of the bored bullet is that the fish can give a good bite indication on the float without having to move the lead—the line slides through the hole in the leger weight without any effort being required by the fish to move it.

For still-water fishing on very rough, windy days, this method is an excellent 'weather beater', as the rod tip can be pushed under the water just after the cast has been made and the line slowly tightened and 'sunk' to beat the surface movement or drift. An antennae float with a very long top stem will ride the waves in a steady fashion for such occasions and the bored bullet will anchor the tackle down securely and stop the float from dragging it around out of the groundbaited area. In order that the line from float to rod tip sinks instantly, it should be rubbed with a small piece of sponge, impregnated with ordinary household detergent (washing-up liquid is fine) and 'back-shotted' by nipping a small split-shot on to the line a foot or so above the float.

Rod Tip and Touch Legering

The most elementary way to leger is to tighten the line up to the weight, then, with the rod in two rests, simply watch the rod tip for bumps and jerks. If legering in the dark, sit quite still, holding the rod, and wait

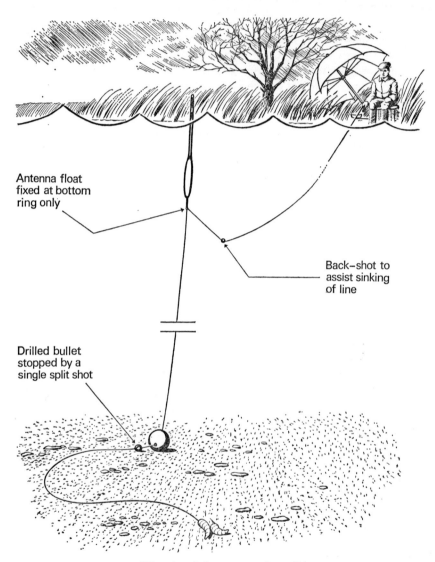

Antenna float
fixed at bottom
ring only

Back–shot to
assist sinking
of line

Drilled bullet
stopped by a
single split shot

45. *'Float leger' for very rough conditions.*

for the bite movements to be transmitted through it. One very sensitive way to do this last method is called 'touch legering'. It requires some practise and lots of concentration, but once mastered it is wonderful for night fishing when non-illuminated visual aids are useless. The basic idea is to sit motionless and comfortable with the rod pointing straight down the line. By holding the line delicately between your thumb and forefinger, you can actually feel any movement or vibration made by a fish picking up or mouthing the bait.

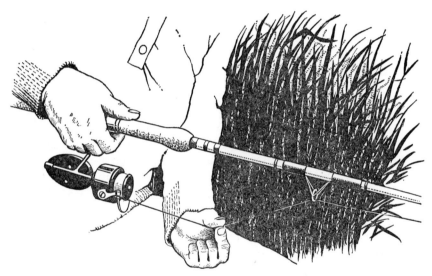

46. *'Touch' legering.*

Dough Bobbin and Silver Paper Indicators

These are quite simple, although the name 'Dough Bobbin' is apt to be misleading for it springs from the days when anglers actually used doughy paste. After casting out with leger gear, they hung a piece of paste on a pulled down loop of line between the reel and the bottom rod ring and watched for a tightening of the line when it jerked up a little. At night, a piece of silver paper or shiny foil will serve the same purpose and it has the advantage of being visible on quite dark nights.

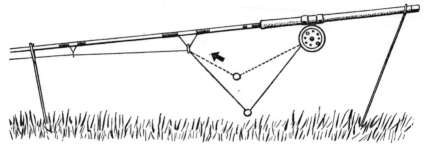

47. *'Dough-bobbin' indicator.*

The 'Swing Tip'

In your observations at the waterside, especially on rivers, you may have seen an angler apparently fishing with a broken rod top that flops and dangles around when he casts or reels in again. However, far from being careless, he is using a swing tip, a most sensitive piece of legering equipment which has recently revolutionized the match angling scene. Swing tips are actually extensions of the rod with a flexible intermediate joint between the two rigid portions (rod top and stiff part of swing tip). They screw into specially designed, threaded rod-tip rings so that the rod can be used in the ordinary way if so desired. When used by an expert their bite registration is truly amazing. After the leger tackle is cast and allowed to settle, the line is tightened so that the swing tip hangs down just above the surface of the water when the rod is mounted almost parallel to the bank edge in two rests. Bite indication is usually of two kinds. Either the swing tip rises sharply and swings upwards like a pendulum when a taking fish pulls at the line, or it falls sharply back, away from the direction of the tackle when the fish picks up the bait and swims towards the rod, slackening the tension off the line.

Quiver Tips

This item of tackle is really a very thin, flexible extension of the rod tip and is screwed into a special threaded top joint ring in the same way as a swing tip. Whereas the swing tip is particularly useful in still waters

48. *Swing tipping (a) The swing tip mounted on rod showing method of bite indication. (b) Position of angler, rod rest and rod when using the swing tip.*

(a)

(b)

and slow flowing rivers or drains, a quiver tip which is very thin but flexible over its whole length, is more appropriate for water with a faster flow. It absorbs some of the water pull and vibrations on the line, but it clearly indicates any undue movement of the terminal tackle which usually denotes attention by a taking fish.

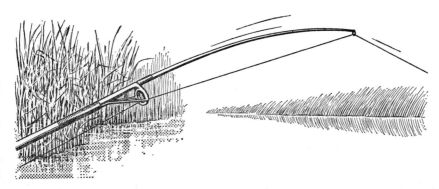

49. *The 'Quiver tip'.*

Rod Butt Bite Indicators

The rod butt bite indicator is very much on the lines of a mechanical 'dough-bobbin' style indicator. It is a very lightweight 'arm' about 9 in. to 12 ins. in length, with a ring through which to pass the line on one end and a spring clip for mounting it on the rod, between the two bottom rings, on the other. It is positioned to point forward, down the rod, with the mounting clip nearest the reel. In practice it hangs down at an angle of about 45 degrees. It is used in conjunction with a leger when the rod is mounted in two rests pointing directly down the line to give a straight pull from terminal tackle to butt indicator.

The very latest style butt indicators can be bought in the form of a special rod butt ring which incorporates a removable hinged indicator arm. The drawback with such an arrangement is that this butt indicator is not interchangeable from one rod to another (the clip-on variety is) as the rod ring to which it is secured must be whipped permanently to one rod.

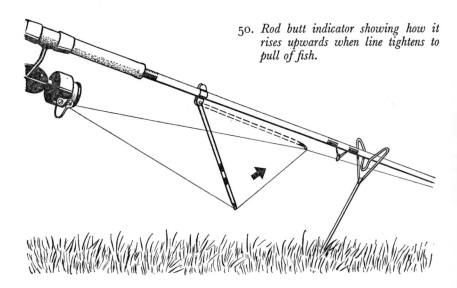

50. *Rod butt indicator showing how it rises upwards when line tightens to pull of fish.*

In very rough water conditions, and when gale force winds are blowing, butt indicators are sometimes the only form of bite indication which can be used effectively. Their position on the rod, very near to the angler, enables them to be sheltered by the umbrella which is keeping the wind off him. After a cast is made, the two rod rests should be positioned so that at least a foot of the rod tip is beneath the water. The whole tackle set-up now ensures that the line is immediately sunk. The rod end does not dance about in the wind or waves, and most important, the butt indicator, being sheltered, only indicates bites and does not dither violently when strong gusts blow.

Do-It-Yourself Rod and Float Kits

Eventually, most anglers with inventive and enquiring minds reach the stage when they require something special as far as rods and floats are concerned. At the present time, the tackle trade are marketing a very wide range of rod kits for 'Do-It-Yourself' enthusiasts. These work out at a price somewhere around half that of the ready-for-use finished article. Rod and float making is not in the least bit difficult. Patience and neatness are the attributes required rather than great skill in the use of tools, and those tools you do need for fashioning rods and floats from ready-made kits are usually to be found in any household shed, garage or tool cupboard.

The great advantage of making your own rods and floats lies in the personal preferences you can allow yourself so far as the finish and finer points of design are concerned. Rods can be 'tailored' to your own taste, so far as length, cork handle thickness, rings, ferrules, colour of whippings, reel fittings and glossy or matt varnish finish are concerned. The float which was your favourite before you lost it and discovered, to your dismay, that it could not be replaced, can be reproduced from an amalgamation of cork, balsa, cane, hardwood dowel or wire. These are all instantly available, often in readily formed shapes from the tackle dealers. Some people's eyes respond to certain colours and the angler will find that he can buy float paints in a wide variety of colours so that he can choose one to suit him and colour all the tips of the floats he makes.

Care of Tackle

Fishing tackle is expensive and it will not stand up to wanton neglect or misuse. The angler who quite cheerfully dumps his gear into the corner of a damp shed or garage and forgets it until the next time he requires it will not be the proud possessor of a sound set of tackle for long. Moisture and grit are the two main enemies which must be instantly removed before tackle is stored until the next outing. Why is it that a strong 'fish dock' aroma surrounds some anglers when they are about to set out for the water before they have been in contact with anything remotely resembling a fish? The answer is ancient fish slime which is still adhering to keep-nets, landing nets and rod handles. Wash these after each outing. The nets under a strong jet of cold running water in the kitchen sink and the rod corks with a soft nail brush and a little soap, ensuring of course, that they are dry and sweet smelling before you put them away again

Bait boxes should be emptied and thoroughly cleaned. Nothing is more revolting for the long suffering tackle dealer than to have a bait box handed to him, with a cheerful request for maggots, only to find when he opens it that a hoard of half dopey blue bottles fills his shop! The bland angler on the other side of the counter forgot all about the maggots he had left over from his last fishing trip—six weeks ago!

Umbrellas need very special care and attention to keep them in good fettle. Moisture is the enemy which destroys them, not the rain which falls whilst you are sheltering thankfully underneath their comforting mushroom shape, but the dampness which you overlook when you think they are thoroughly dry and roll them up. I once had the occasion to borrow a brolly which had been sadly neglected. As the rain clouds gathered and the first drops pattered down, I opened it up. To say it was mildewed would be a gross understatement. It actually had a very thick growth of fungus upon it which had eaten right into the fabric and made it rotten. Much to my disgust, it leaked like a sieve and I felt as though I was sitting under a shower bath the whole day.

The bottoms of rod holdalls are apt to collect moisture from dripping umbrellas, wet rod bags and landing-net heads. Quite often the trouble is unsuspected until the fateful day when the bottom falls out, due to rotting stitches. Empty your holdall after each angling trip and blow a hairdryer down it for ten minutes or so, with the warm air switch on. It works wonders and extends the life of these costly items by many years.

A final point on the security aspect of fishing tackle. As I stressed earlier, it is expensive and if you have a very exclusive collection it is irreplaceable. Therefore, make sure you store it in a very safe place. Not in a garage where the doors are liable to be left open or in an insecure outhouse or shed where if thieves don't get it, rats or mice will. Nothing less than a good dry cupboard or spare room indoors will do. You may possibly chuckle with mirth, but I know one ardent angler—a bachelor naturally—who smilingly lies back in bed and views his treasured rods in racks all around the bedroom walls. Cupboards full of reels and other tackle are built-in underneath them. His basket is safely tucked away under the bed and two large plastic bins, full of a very special, secret groundbait stand by the door. Security indeed!

INDEX

Lilian Rubin, M.A.

Note: An asterisk denotes an illustration

Roach

Rudd

Dace

Chub

Perch

Eel

Barbel